PMP Exam Prep Seminar Participant Workbook

Published by
Instructing.com, LL

For 35-contact hours of project management education, PDUs, or on-site training please visit: www.instructing.com.

Updated October 9, 2016; Version 5.1

Earn Your PMP Certification

PMBOK V, PROJECTS, AND THE PMP EXAM

This PMP Exam Prep Workbook will walk you through the entire *PMBOK Guide, fifth edition* and all of the PMP Exam objectives. Throughout the book you'll see PMBOK numbering references in the slide headlines. You will also see an occasional activity to perform. If you're in a study group or self-led training endeavor use this workbook to organize your notes as you prepare to pass. Make certain you're familiar with everything in this book - including the PMP Memory Sheets provided as the last several pages.

If you need your 35 contact hours of education visit us at www.instructing.com. We offer a 35-hour PMP Exam Prep seminar online. And since you've purchased this book use the code **PMPWBOOK** to save $50 on the 35-hour course.

If you've questions or comments please contact us: cs@instructing.com. Thanks! All the best in your projects.

Always check with PMI for complete exam details:

http://www.pmi.org/certifications/types/project-management-pmp

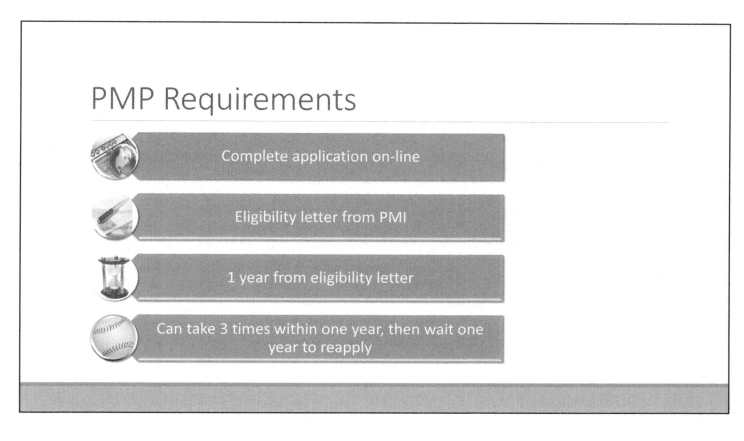

PMP Requirements

- Complete application on-line
- Eligibility letter from PMI
- 1 year from eligibility letter
- Can take 3 times within one year, then wait one year to reapply

Learning is hard work, but your goal is to work smart, not just hard. The PMP exam is founded on the Project Management Institute (PMI) book, *A Guide to the Project Management Body of Knowledge, fifth edition* (hereafter referred to as the *PMBOK Guide*). If you want to pass the PMP exam, you'll first need to qualify for the exam and then create a plan on how to pass the test. Let's get that part straight right away – your goal is pass the test. Your goal isn't to take the test. Your goal isn't to get a perfect score. Your goal is to simply pass the test.

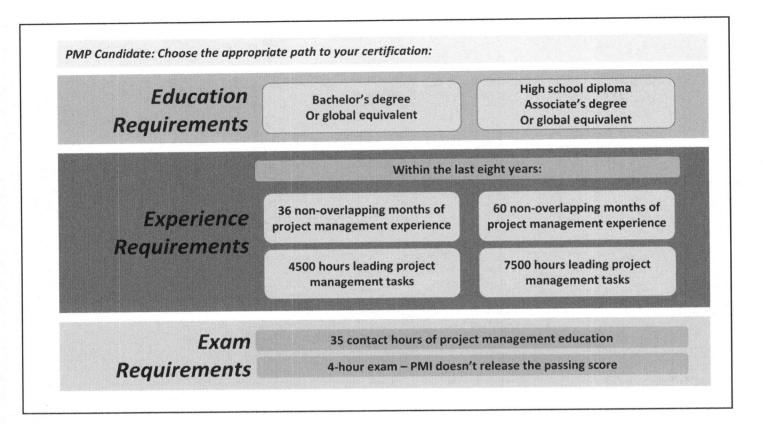

PMP Candidate: Choose the appropriate path to your certification:

Education Requirements	Bachelor's degree Or global equivalent	High school diploma Associate's degree Or global equivalent
Experience Requirements	**Within the last eight years:**	
	36 non-overlapping months of project management experience	60 non-overlapping months of project management experience
	4500 hours leading project management tasks	7500 hours leading project management tasks
Exam Requirements	35 contact hours of project management education	
	4-hour exam – PMI doesn't release the passing score	

In order to pass the test you'll *basically* need to answer 106 questions correctly out of 175. Wait a minute! The PMP exam, as everyone knows, has 200 questions – not 175 questions. Correct! But, the PMP exam has 25 seeded questions, which PMI calls pre-test questions. These questions aren't pre-test for you; they are pre-test questions that haven't yet been added to the possible pool of PMP questions.

Based on how PMP candidates answer these questions, PMI will judge if the questions are too easy, too hard, or just ridiculous enough to be added to the pool of questions for future exam takers. On your test these seeded questions are sprinkled among the 175 questions that do count towards your passing score. You won't know if you're answering a pre-test question or a live question so you have to answer all of the questions with the same intensity.

PMP Exam Fees

$405 per PMI member

$555 per non-PMI member

$129 to join PMI

After the PMP

Celebrate

Earning PDUs

Share your story

Complete the Application Online

www.pmi.org

Can start, stop, and save your application

Complete the application ASAP – don't wait!

If you've not yet completed your PMP application on PMI's website do it now. It's not a quick application and can take some time to get approved by PMI. Let them work on the approval process while you're preparing to pass. No need to do a month's of preparation only to come to a grinding halt to fill out the exam application. Once your application has been approved you will immediately, yes, immediately schedule your exam. Create a deadline to work towards.

_____

_____

_____

_____

_____

_____

_____

Certificate of Course Completion

Given at the end of the PMP Exam Prep Seminar

Only need the certificate if you're audited

Complete entire course to claim application

Name on application and certificate of completion

Info to provide:
- Institution name: Instructing.com, LLC
- REP Info: #4082
- Contact hours of course: 35 contact hours
- Instructor: Joseph Phillips, PMP

Activity: Start Your PMP Application

Visit www.pmi.org

Click "Certifications"

Choose Project Management Professional

Choose Apply for PMP Certification

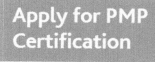

Apply for PMP Certification

Register and log in to get started

APPLY NOW

If you've not yet completed your PMP application on PMI's website, do it now. It's not a quick application and can take some time to get approved by PMI. Let them work on the approval process while you're preparing to pass. No need to do a month of study only to come to a grinding halt to fill out the exam application.

ACTIVITY: CREATE A STUDY STRATEGY

STUDY TO PASS THE EXAM – NOT JUST TAKE THE EXAM

You have to pass the exam within one year of being approved, but you won't need anywhere need that much time. For what it's worth, I know several project managers who went through the process and chickened out and never scheduled their exam. Procrastination will kill you on this effort. You're going to pass the PMP exam; set a deadline and make it happen.

_____

_____

_____

_____

_____

_____

_____

Your Goal is to Pass the PMP

What's your schedule like?

Can you offer one, two, or four hours every day?

My recommendation is to take the exam sooner rather than later

The longer you wait…

Create a Place to Learn

Emulate the exam environment

Quiet, no distractions
- Emails
- Texts
- Visitors

Two hours of quiet time

Immerse yourself in the PMP

You'll also need a place to study. This means somewhere quiet, uninterrupted, clean, and well-lit. If you're lucky enough to have a home office, there you go. I've worked other PMPs who didn't have that luxury so they commandeered an after-work conference room, space in a library, and I know of more than one PMP who hunkered down in a rented cabin for a week to study and be unreachable. Find a solution that works for you – but you'll need a PMP Exam Study Headquarters. Clean, well-lit, distraction-free are all ways to describe your exam headquarters.

_____

_____

_____

_____

_____

_____

_____

Complete the Course

Take the course in any order you like

Take notes as you move through the course

Review your notes before leaving a module

Ask questions! Use the discussion feature

Know What to Study

14 Chapters to Study

Real exam focus in on Chapters 4 through 10

- Integration management
- Scope
- Time
- Cost
- Quality
- Human Resources
- Communications
- Risk
- Procurement
- Stakeholders

Whatever schedule you create you must adhere to. No, you can't study later. No, you can't browse Reddit for pictures of kittens. No, you can't watch your favorite episode of Matlock. If you want to pass the test you must create and stick to the schedule. Study everyday at the same time. I recommend you study at the same time for when you've schedule your exam – might as well get your brain in PMP mode.

How long to study? One hour to four hours at a time if you're doing a monthly schedule. If you're taking the two-week approach you'll dig in and immerse yourself in the materials. Alternate four hours to six hours one day, and then break up the next day with smaller segments of review.

_____

_____

_____

_____

_____

_____

_____

_____

Sample Four-Week Study Strategy

Week One: Complete the PMP Exam Prep Seminar

Week Two - Focus on:
- Module 5: Scope
- Module 6: Time
- Module 7: Cost
- Module 8: Quality
- Module 9: HR

Week Three - Focus on:
- Module 10: Communications
- Module 11: Risk
- Module 12: Procurement
- Module 13: Stakeholder Management

Sample Four-Week Study Strategy

Week Four: Put it all together
- Take all practice exams until you can score 100 percent
- Review flashcards until the are perfect every time
- Practice creating exam memory sheets

I'm often asked how long should it take to pass the PMP? Well, technically you only have four hours to pass the test, but you can prepare to pass the PMP in four weeks. Four weeks?! Absolutely!

_____

_____

_____

_____

_____

_____

_____

_____

Activity: Building Your Study Strategy

Create a realistic plan
- Treat it like a project
- Schedule the work
- Execute your plan

Dedicate yourself to the project

Don't stretch this out too long

"Success means doing the best we can with what we have. Success is the doing, not the getting; in the trying, not the triumph. Success is a personal standard, reaching for the highest that is in us, becoming all that we can be."

– Zig Ziglar

CONSIDER THE PMP APPLICATION AUDIT

YOUR APPLICATION COULD BE AUDITED BY PMI

There's much concern and some confusion regarding the PMP exam application. Some folks will tell you that if you're "real careful" with your wording you won't get audited. Other people tell you that's it order of your projects that affect the audit outcome. The truth is, as I explain in this lecture, the audit selection process is actually totally random. There's nothing you can do to totally avoid an audit of your application.

Why does PMI Audit Applications?

Confirms education and experience

Enhances the credibility of the certification

Filter out "paper" project managers

PMP Application Audit Truth

There's only one way to avoid an audit:

- Don't apply for the exam

A small percentage of applications are randomly audited

Audits are Random

You can't avoid the chance of an audit

It's random – not profiling

It's a small chance that you'll be audited

_____

_____

_____

_____

_____

_____

_____

_____

What's the audit like?

Verify education experience
- Photocopy of your degree or transcripts
- Proof of course completion

Verify project management experience
- Your project experience becomes a PDF doc
- Project supervisors will have to sign what you wrote
- Envelope also signed across the back seal

Mail all documents back to PMI Headquarters

PDUS OR CONTACT HOURS?

LEARNING THE DIFFERENCE BETWEEN THE TWO...

Contact hours and PDUs are not the same thing! You get contact hours before you are a PMP. Once you're a PMP, then you can earn PDUs... this lecture explains the difference.

This lecture also explains the new PMI Talent Triangle and how your PDUs are distributed among technology, leadership, and business.

_____

_____

_____

_____

_____

_____

_____

_____

What is a contact hour?

Contact hours are:
- Project management education hours
- Happen before your exam application
- Must cover project management materials
- This course qualifies you for 35 contact hours

What is a PDU?

PDUs are:
- Professional Development Units
- Happen after your exam
- PMPs need 60 every three years
- One hour of education is one PDU

2015 PMI PDU Requirement

Effective December 1, 2015

35 minimum education PDUs

25 maximum "giving back" PDUs

PMI Talent Triangle Requirement

Technical project management: 8 PDUs

Leadership: 8 PDUs

Business & Strategic Management: 8 PDUs

Combination from any three areas: 11 PDUs

Total of 35 minimum educational PDUs

Right now you don't have to worry too much about the PMI Talent Triangle. After you pass the PMP, however, you'll be more concerned with your PDUs and the Talent Triangle.

Basically, once you're a PMP you have to distribute your PDUs earned in leadership, business and strategic management, and technical PDUs for a minimum of 35 educational PDUs. You can get all of your PDUs from classes and seminars, but you'll need to have 35 of the PDUs distributed as in the above slide. In other words, you can't claim 60 PDUs only from technical project management.

Giving Back PDUs

25 Maximum PDUs

Creating new knowledge

Volunteering

Working as project professional (8 PDU max)

"There are two types of people who will tell you that you cannot make a difference in this world: those who are afraid to try and those who are afraid you will succeed."

— Ray Goforth

Focus on Passing Exam, Not PDUs

Post-exam focus on PDUs

Look for my training

All PDUs from education is fine

First things first... pass the PMP!

UTILIZE THE COURSE RESOURCES

GETTING RESOURCES TO HELP YOUR STUDY EFFORTS

If you're taking this course as part of Instructing.com's online learning, then the next few pages will make perfect sense to you.

If you're using this book as a study-aid or in a study group these next few "slides" won't mean much to you.

If you're using this book in an instructor-led PMP Exam Prep Seminar your instructor will explain how best to participate in your course.

Flashcards

Create flashcards based on PMP terms from PMBOK and other resources

Online course: flashcards provided in PDF format

Buzz through the terms every day

Knowing the terms will help you answer questions correctly

It's been said that repetition is the mother of learning. These PMP Exam Prep Flashcards will help you learn all of the project management terms - and that'll make passing the PMP Exam even easier. There are three sets of flashcards included:

One term per page - great for studying flashcards on your phone

Two terms per page - great for printing or viewing on a tablet computer

Three terms per page - ideal for printing all of the terms to study unplugged

_____

_____

_____

_____

_____

_____

_____

Using the Memory Sheets

Included as a resource
- PDF
- Participant workbook

You must know everything on these memory sheets

At the start of the exam recreate your memorized memory sheets

Formulas, theories, and other concepts

These PMP Memory Sheets include everything you must know for your PMI exam. Inside this lecture and document you'll find secrets to help you pass the PMP exam. This document includes details on these key PMP Exam topics:

- Project integration management
- Tips for finding float
- Schedule management for all projects
- Project cost estimating and budgeting
- Earned value management formulas
- Quality control and quality assurance
- Human resources on the project team
- Communication terms you must know for your PMP exam
- How to identify, analyze, and respond to project risks
- Following the procurement processes
- Stakeholder management tips and secrets
- All of the PMP processes in knowledge areas and in process groups

The exam memory sheets are part of this workbook. The memory sheets are the final pages of this workbook.

Participant Workbook

Follows the online course

PDF document from online course

Universal project management workbook: self-led, instructor-led, or online learning

_____

_____

_____

_____

_____

_____

_____

Other Resources

Online course

Instructor-led course

Resources external to this course

Respect the intellectual rights of others

EXPLORE THE PMBOK GUIDE

A GUIDE TO THE PROJECT MANAGEMENT BODY OF KNOWLEDGE

Yes, you need to study the *PMBOK Guide*, for your exam. If you've selected some other materials to help you along the *PMBOK Guide* can serve as a good reference point for your materials. If you're reading the *PMBOK Guide* straight-up, well, it's pretty boring. It reads like a toaster manual and isn't always easy to comprehend.

The *PMBOK Guide*, however, is what your exam is based upon, so I do recommend you have a copy on hand. Within the *PMBOK Guide* you'll need to know all that you can about the project management processes. This isn't just memorizing the 47 project management processes, but rather understanding how to apply the processes in a given scenario.

1.1 Purpose of the PMBOK Guide

Generally recognized approach to project management

Describes good practice for project management

Common lexicon of project management terms

Fundamental for PMI Exams:

- PMP
- CAPM
- PgMP
- PMI-ACP
- PMI-RMP
- PMI-SP

The application of the processes often trips up would-be PMPs. For example, if you never get the chance to procure anything in your projects because all of the vendor management is handled outside of the project, then the procurement chapter may be real tough for you. The same is true with any of the different processes. While you personally may not have experience with all 47 project management processes, you must understand how all of the processes work in a project. This is why the preparation is tricky and takes time and effort.

All About the PMBOK Guide

A Guide to the Project Management Body of Knowledge

13 chapters

PMP exam and the PMBOK Guide

Five process groups

47 processes

Ten knowledge areas

Did you know that if you join PMI you can access an electronic copy of the *PMBOK Guide*? It's true! So, if you want to manage your funds, considering the cost of the exam, you could join PMI, save a bit on your exam fee and access the *PMBOK Guide* as a PDF document.

I actually prefer the electronic version because I can use the search feature to find keywords for questions, review, and geeky project management trivia.

PMBOK Chapters

Chapter 1: Introduction

Chapter 2: Organizational Influences and Project Life Cycle

Chapter 3: Project Management Processes

PMBOK Chapters

Chapter 4: Project Integration Management

Chapter 5: Project Scope Management

Chapter 6: Project Time Management

Chapter 7: Project Cost Management

Chapter 8: Project Quality Management

PMBOK Sections

Chapter 9: Project Human Resource Management

Chapter 10: Project Communications Management

Chapter 11: Project Risk Management

Chapter 12: Project Procurement Management

Chapter 13: Project Stakeholder Management

EXPLORE THE PMBOK GUIDE

A GUIDE TO THE PROJECT MANAGEMENT BODY OF KNOWLEDGE

There are eight initiating tasks for the 2016 PMP exam. Initiating accounts for 13 percent of the PMP exam and has two new tasks for the exam.

_____

_____

_____

_____

_____

_____

_____

_____

Tasks for Initiating

Perform project assessment based upon available information, lessons learned from previous projects, and meetings with relevant stakeholders in order to support the evaluation of the feasibility of new products or services within the given assumptions and/or constraints.

_____

_____

_____

_____

_____

_____

_____

_____

Tasks for Initiating

Identify key deliverables based on the business requirements in order to manage customer expectations and direct the achievement of project goals.

Tasks for Initiating

Perform stakeholder analysis using appropriate tools and techniques in order to align expectations and gain support for the project.

Tasks for Initiating

Identify high level risks, assumptions, and constraints based on the current environment, organizational factors, historical data, and expert judgment, in order to propose an implementation strategy.

"Things may come to those who wait, but only the things left by those who hustle."

– Abraham Lincoln

Tasks for Initiating

Participate in the development of the project charter by compiling and analyzing gathered information in order to ensure project stakeholders are in agreement on its elements.

Tasks for Initiating

Obtain project charter approval from the sponsor, in order to formalize the authority assigned to the project manager and gain commitment and acceptance for the project.

Tasks for Initiating

Conduct benefit analysis with relevant stakeholders to validate project alignment with organizational strategy and expected business value.

_____

_____

_____

_____

_____

_____

_____

Tasks for Initiating

Inform stakeholders of the approved project charter to ensure common understanding of the key deliverables, milestones, and their roles and responsibilities.

PLAN THE PROJECT: EXAM DOMAIN II OVERVIEW

PLANNING: 24 PERCENT OF PMP EXAM

13 PLANNING TASKS

The PMP exam domain Planning accounts for 24 percent of the PMP exam. There are 13 planning tasks covered in this domain. There is only one new task in this domain.

_____

_____

_____

_____

_____

_____

_____

Tasks for Planning

Review and assess detailed project requirements, constraints, and assumptions with stakeholders based on the project charter, lessons learned, and by using requirement gathering techniques in order to establish detailed project deliverables.

_____

_____

_____

_____

_____

_____

_____

Tasks for Planning

Develop a scope management plan, based on the approved project scope and using scope management techniques, in order to define, maintain, and manage the scope of the project.

Tasks for Planning

Develop the cost management plan based on the project scope, schedule, resources, approved project charter and other information, using estimating techniques, in order to manage project costs.

Tasks for Planning

Develop the project schedule based on the approved project deliverables and milestones, scope, and resource management plans in order to manage timely completion of the project.

Tasks for Planning

Develop the human resource management plan by defining the roles and responsibilities of the project team members in order to create a project organizational structure and provide guidance regarding how resources will be assigned and managed.

Tasks for Planning

Develop the communications management plan based on the project organizational structure and stakeholder requirements, in order to define and manage the flow of project information.

"Never limit yourself because of others' limited imagination; never limit others because of your own limited imagination."

— Mae Jemison

Tasks for Planning

Develop the procurement management plan based on the project scope, budget, and schedule, in order to ensure that the required project resources will be available.

Tasks for Planning

Develop the quality management plan and define the quality standards for the project and its products, based on the project scope, risks, and requirements, in order to prevent the occurrence of defects and control the cost of quality.

_____

_____

_____

_____

_____

_____

_____

Tasks for Planning

Develop the change management plan by defining how changes will be addressed and controlled in order to track and manage change.

Tasks for Planning

Plan for risk management by developing a risk management plan; identifying, analyzing, and prioritizing project risk; creating the risk register; and defining risk response strategies in order to manage uncertainty and opportunity throughout the project life cycle.

Tasks for Planning

Present the project management plan to the relevant stakeholders according to applicable policies and procedures in order to obtain approval to proceed with project execution.

Tasks for Planning

Conduct kick-off meeting, communicating the start of the project, key milestones, and other relevant information in order to inform and engage stakeholders and gain commitment.

Tasks for Planning

Develop the stakeholder management plan by analyzing needs, interests, and potential impact in order to effectively manage stakeholders' expectations and engage them in project decisions.

EXECUTE THE PROJECT: EXAM DOMAIN III OVERVIEW

EXECUTING: 31 PERCENT OF PMP EXAM

7 EXECUTING TASKS

The PMP exam domain of Executing accounts for 31 percent of the PMP exam. There are seven executing tasks covered in this domain, two of which are new tasks.

_____

_____

_____

_____

_____

_____

_____

_____

Tasks for Executing

Acquire and manage project resources by following the human resource and procurement management plans in order to meet project requirements.

_____

_____

_____

_____

_____

_____

_____

_____

Tasks for Executing

Manage task execution based on the project management plan by leading and developing the project team in order to achieve project deliverables.

Tasks for Executing

Implement the quality management plan using the appropriate tools and techniques in order to ensure that work is performed in accordance with required quality standards.

"Success does not consist in never making mistakes but in never making the same one a second time."

— George Bernard Shaw

Tasks for Executing

Implement approved changes and corrective actions by following the change management plan in order to meet project requirements.

Tasks for Executing

Implement approved actions by following the risk management plan in order to minimize the impact of the risks and take advantage of opportunities on the project.

_____

_____

_____

_____

_____

_____

_____

Tasks for Executing

Manage the flow of information by following the communications plan in order to keep stakeholders engaged and informed.

_____

_____

_____

_____

_____

_____

_____

_____

Tasks for Executing

Maintain stakeholder relationships by following the stakeholder management plan in order to receive continued support and manage expectations.

MONITOR AND CONTROL THE PROJECT: EXAM DOMAIN IV OVERVIEW

MONITORING & CONTROLLING: 25 PERCENT OF PMP EXAM

7 MONITORING & CONTROLLING TASKS

The Monitoring and Controlling PMP Exam domain accounts for 25 percent of the exam. There are seven monitoring and controlling tasks in this domain - two of which are new.

Tasks for Monitoring and Controlling

Measure project performance using appropriate tools and techniques in order to identify and quantify any variances and corrective actions.

Tasks for Monitoring and Controlling

Manage changes to the project by following the change management plan in order to ensure that project goals remain aligned with business needs.

Tasks for Monitoring and Controlling

Verify that project deliverables conform to the quality standards established in the quality management plan by using appropriate tools and techniques to meet project requirements and business needs.

Tasks for Monitoring and Controlling

Monitor and assess risk by determining whether exposure has changed and evaluating the effectiveness of response strategies in order to manage the impact of risks and opportunities on the project.

Tasks for Monitoring and Controlling

Review the issue log, update if necessary, and determine corrective actions by using appropriate tools and techniques in order to minimize the impact on the project.

Tasks for Monitoring and Controlling

Capture, analyze, and manage lessons learned, using lessons learned management techniques in order to enable continuous improvement.

> *"Success means having the courage, the determination, and the will to become the person you believe you were meant to be."*
>
> *— George Sheehan*

Tasks for Monitoring and Controlling

Monitor procurement activities according to the procurement plan in order to verify compliance with project objectives.

CLOSE THE PROJECT: EXAM DOMAIN V OVERVIEW

CLOSING: 7 PERCENT OF PMP EXAM

7 CLOSING TASKS

The 2016 PMP exam domain of closing accounts for seven percent of the PMP exam domain and has seven closing tasks. No new tasks have been added to this domain.

_____

_____

_____

_____

_____

_____

_____

Tasks for Closing

Obtain final acceptance of the project deliverables from relevant stakeholders in order to confirm that project scope and deliverables were achieved.

Tasks for Closing

Transfer the ownership of deliverables to the assigned stakeholders in accordance with the project plan in order to facilitate project closure.

Tasks for Closing

Obtain financial, legal, and administrative closure using generally accepted practices and policies in order to communicate formal project closure and ensure transfer of liability.

Tasks for Closing

Prepare and share the final project report according to the communications management plan in order to document and convey project performance and assist in project evaluation.

Tasks for Closing

Collate lessons learned that were documented throughout the project and conduct a comprehensive project review in order to update the organization's knowledge base.

Tasks for Closing

Archive project documents and materials using generally accepted practices in order to comply with statutory requirements and for potential use in future projects and audits.

Tasks for Closing

Obtain feedback from relevant stakeholders using appropriate tools and techniques and based on the stakeholder management plan in order to evaluate their satisfaction.

Activity: Download the PMP Assets

1. Visit www.pmi.org
2. Click Certifications
3. Choose Project Management Professional
4. Download Exam Content Outline
5. PMP Handbook

PMP Exam Guidance

Review tips, resources and FAQs to help you prepare.

Downloads

Exam Content Outline 🗎

Handbook 🗎

DEFINE PROJECT BASICS

STARTING WITH A GOOD FOUNDATION OF PROJECT MANAGEMENT

In order to be a project manager you need to understand what a project is, what a project manager does, and how your personality can help you be a better project manager. Consider:
- The difference between projects and operations
- Management skills you'll need
- Using your personality

_____

_____

_____

_____

_____

_____

_____

1.2 What is a Project?

Temporary endeavor
- Definite beginning and end

Creates a unique product, service, or result

Projects can involve:
- A single person
- A single organizational unit
- Multiple organizational units

A project is a temporary undertaking to create something unique – think of a new product, a new service, or even a new condition in your organization. Two interesting words in that last sentence when it comes to projects: temporary and unique. Temporary, of course, means that it won't last forever. The reason I'm stressing temporary is that's one of the first realizations of a project versus an operation. Consider the manufacturing of a new car – that's, for all practical purposes, an on-going operation. The design and creation of the car to be manufactured, however, is a project. It has a clear beginning and a clear ending. Projects do not last forever (they may feel that they do), but have a definite beginning and a definite end.

The second word is unique. A project creates something that has never, ever, been created before. You say, "Slow down there, professor. I've managed lots of projects that have created the same thing over and over." That's probably true to some extent: a construction company may build the same model home over and over. An IT consulting firm may install the same piece of software over and over. And even a cake designer may create the same type of cake over and over. The point is every one of those homes, software installs, and yummy cakes are unique.

1.2 Projects Create...

An item, an enhancement, or a component of another item

Service or capability to perform a service

Improvement in an existing item

Result – outcome or document

1.2.1 Relationships Among Portfolios, Programs, and Projects

Coordinated, orchestrated effort for organizational goals

Strategies and prioritization

Common governance

Uniform change control

Performance measurement

1.3 What is Project Management?

Application of knowledge, skills, tools, and techniques
to meet the project requirements

47 project management processes

Five project management process groups
- Initiating
- Planning
- Executing
- Monitoring and Controlling
- Closing

Project management begins with an idea – and usually not the project manager's idea – of something that needs to be done, created, removed, or invented. The idea itself usually comes from a stakeholder. You might know your stakeholders as management, customers, or end users. A stakeholder is simply a person that has a vested interest in the outcome of your project. Technically speaking, the idea is really about the product that your project will be creating.

_____

_____

_____

_____

_____

_____

_____

1.3 Typical Project Management

Identifying requirements

Addressing needs, concerns, and expectations of stakeholders

Setting up, maintaining, and carrying out communications

Managing stakeholders

Balancing competing project constraints:
- Scope,
- Quality,
- Schedule,
- Budget,
- Resources, and Risks

1.3 Progressive Elaboration

Idea or Concept

Formulate the idea

Business Case

Feasibility Study

Project

Project Management Application Areas

 Construction

 Health Care

 Government

 Information technology

MANAGE PROJECTS AND THE ORGANIZATION

PROJECTS CAN EXIST IN MANY DIFFERENT ORGANIZATIONAL TYPES

Chances are projects within your organization are of the same nature. What I mean by that is that you and your fellow project managers are probably managing projects that have something in common: you are all managing IT projects, managing health care projects, construction projects, and so on. The industry that you work in is the application area and your projects happen within that application area.

Your projects likely also have something else in common – they exist to support something more than just the project. Your projects exist to help your organization, your company, your community, increase revenue, decrease costs, improve a condition, or support an idea or service. Projects, for all intensive purposes, serve some greater good.

_____

_____

_____

_____

_____

_____

_____

Portfolio Management, Program Management, Project Management, and Organizational Project Management

Table 1-1 in PMBOK Guide, 5th Edition

- Scope
- Change
- Planning
- Management
- Success factors
- Monitoring

Portfolios are about maximizing return on investment

_____

_____

_____

_____

_____

_____

_____

_____

Projects, Programs, and Portfolios

Management and oversight of:
- Scope
- Changes
- Planning
- Management
- Success
- Monitoring

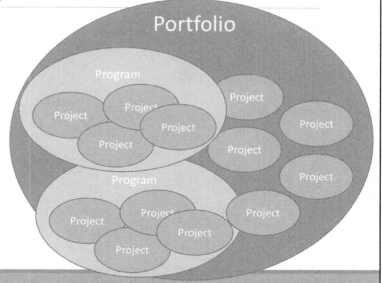

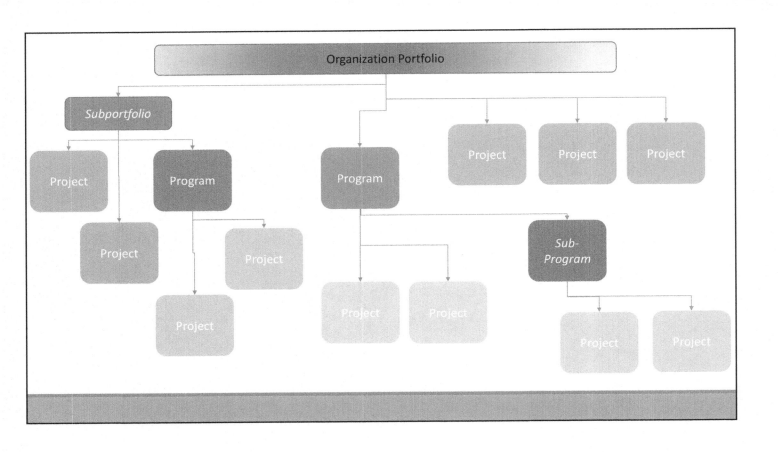

1.4.1 Program Management

Multiple related projects

Achieve benefits

Program managers and project managers

PgMP

1.4.3 Projects and Strategic Planning

Market demands

Opportunities

Social need

Environmental considerations

Customer request

Technological advance

Legal requirements

1.4.4 Project Management Offices

Support project managers

Manage shared resources across the PMO

Coaching, mentoring, and training

Conducting project audits

Developing and managing processes and procedures

Facilitating communications across projects

Not every performing organization has a project management office, but the PMO is a stakeholder if one exists. A PMO is a centralized business unit that oversees all project management activities within an organization, company, or even a department. PMOs are to assist the project managers with scheduling, resource management, training, and more. They are fine people.

_____

_____

_____

_____

_____

_____

_____

_____

1.4.4 Project Management Office Types

Standards project management for an organization

- Supportive – consultative role, templates, training
- Controlling – compliance through a framework, specific forms and templates, governance
- Directive – directly manages the project as the PMO owns and controls the project life cycle

Projects and Strategic Planning

Pyramid diagram:

- **Executives** — Why? Vision, Mission, Goals
- **Functional Management** — What? Strategy and Tactics
- **Operations** — How? LOB, Core Functions

1.5 Projects and Operations

Projects are temporary

- Developing new products or services
- Moving, Adding, Changing, or Deleting
- Implementing new service or solution

Operations are ongoing

- Repetitive actions
- Maintenance
- Core business functions

1.5 Relationship Between Projects, Operations, and Organizational Strategy

Operations and project management

Closeout or end of project phase

Product development

Improving operational processes and life cycles

Product life cycle

Knowledge transfer

1.5.2 Organizations and Project Management

Project-based organizations

Project management and organizational governance

Projects and organizational strategy

Culture

1.6 Business Value

Entire value of the business

Tangible elements
- Monetary assets
- Fixtures and equipment
- Equity

Intangible elements
- Reputation
- Brand recognition
- Trademarks

ESTABLISH THE PROJECT MANAGEMENT ROLE AND RESPONSIBILITIES

WHAT PROJECT MANAGERS DO

You'll be tested on the role of the project manager, the stakeholder-project manager relationships, and how projects operate in organizations. Stakeholder management is a new knowledge area in the *PMBOK Guide*, fifth edition, so you can expect many questions on stakeholder management throughout the exam.

- Working with senior project managers
- Working with programs
- Working with a project management office
- Using enterprise environmental factors

1.7 Role of the Project Manager

Lead the team to achieve the project objectives

Balance the competing objectives of the project

Communicate with stakeholders

Contribute to business value

So where does that put you? Are you a brand new project manager looking for the path of least resistance to project success? Are you a project manager by default looking for the way projects should be perfectly managed in an imperfect world? Or are you a seasoned project manager looking for better approaches, new ideas, or clarifications of project management terms and processes?

Wherever you're coming from, whatever your reason for reading, welcome. I won't pull any punches. I'm going to tell you the way projects should operate, the processes that projects can use – not must use. In this guide I'll detail all of the project management processes that you're likely to use at some point in your life as a project manager. In this guide I'll detail all of the project management processes that you can use to move your project from right now to some point in the future. I'll offer real world, practical advice on managing your project quickly, accurately, and with precision.

_____

_____

_____

_____

_____

_____

_____

1.7.1 Responsibilities and Competencies of the Project Manager

Satisfy task needs, team needs, and individual needs

Liaison between the project team and the business strategy

Three values of a project manager:
- Knowledge: understanding project management
- Performance: accomplish as a project manager
- Personal: behavior, effectiveness, character, leadership

1.7.1 General Management Skills

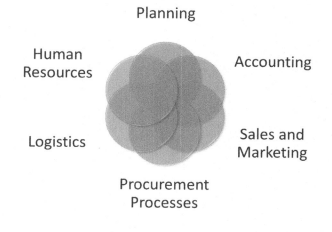

Planning

Human
Resources

Accounting

Logistics

Sales and
Marketing

Procurement
Processes

1.7.2 Interpersonal Skills

Problem solving

Motivating

Communicating

Influencing the organization

Leadership

Negotiating

> *"I cannot give you the formula for success, but I can give you the formula for failure which is: Try to please everybody."*
>
> *— Herbert B. Swope*

Learning Game!

http://www.instructing.com/wp-content/pub/1/story.html

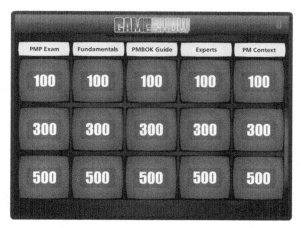

Chapter exam

ORGANIZATIONAL INFLUENCE AND PROJECT LIFE CYCLE

POWER IS INFLUENCED BY YOUR ORGANIZATIONAL STRUCTURE
& THE PROJECT LIFE CYCLE IS UNIQUE TO THE PROJECT

Stakeholders can influence how smoothly your project operates. Depending on the structure your project is operating in you will manage and influence the stakeholders differently. It's important for the PMP exam to recognize the different organizational types and how the project manager may operate within each structure.

The PMP exam will test your understanding of how project managers get things done in different types of organizations.

- Influencing the organization
- How organizations operate
- Considering the organizational structure

2.1 Organizational Influences on Project Management

Organizational cultures and styles

Organizational communications

Structure of the organization

2.1.1 Organizational Culture

Values

Business model

Policies, methods, and processes

View of authority

Work ethic and work hours

While people complete projects, projects are done within organizations. These organizations, not-for-profit or otherwise, have cultures, styles, and values that affect how the project is managed and eventually completed.

_____

_____

_____

_____

_____

_____

_____

2.1.3 Organizational Structures

Affects power of project manager

Affects decision-making abilities

Affects communication demands

Affects project team management

Affects stakeholder management

2.1.3 Organizational Structures and Project Management Power

1	Projectized
2	Strong Matrix
3	Balanced Matrix
4	Weak Matrix
5	Functional

Organizational Structures Detail

	Functional	Weak Matrix	Balanced Matrix	Strong Matrix	Projectized
Project Manager's Authority	Little	Limited	Low to Moderate	Moderate to High	High to Almost Total
Resource Availability	Little	Limited	Low to Moderate	Moderate to High	High to Almost Total
Budget Control	Functional	Functional	Mixed	Project Manager	Project Manager
Project Manager's Role	Part-time	Part-time	Full-time	Full-time	Full-time
Admin Staff	Part-time	Part-time	Part-time	Full-time	Full-time

DESCRIBE ORGANIZATIONAL FACTORS

ENTERPRISE ENVIRONMENTAL FACTORS, ORGANIZATIONAL PROCESS ASSETS, AND OTHER PROJECT ELEMENTS

2.1.4 Organizational Process Assets

Come from
- Process and procedures (historical)
- Corporate knowledge base (prepared)

Historical or prepared
- Past projects
- Lessons learned
- Processes and procedures
- Corporate knowledge base
- Guidelines and accepted practices

2.1.4.2 Corporate Knowledge Base

Configuration management knowledge

Financial databases: labor hours, incurred costs, budgets, and any project cost overruns;

Historical information and lessons learned knowledge bases

Issue and defect management databases

Process measurement databases

Project files from previous projects

2.1.5 Enterprise Environmental Factors

Organizational policies

Industry standards and regulations

Rules that the project manager must abide by

Processes that must be followed

Geographic distribution of facilities

Marketplace conditions

Standards and Regulations

Standards are optional

Regulations are not

2.2 Project Stakeholders and Governance

Interested parties in the project's existence

Affected by the project

Can affect the project

Project team

Project manager

2.2.1 Project Stakeholders

Anyone who's affected by the project

Positive stakeholders

Negative stakeholders

Neutral stakeholders

The people interested in the outcome of your project are called stakeholders. These folks vary in their influence over the project from casual observer to the guy calling the shots and signing the checks. Stakeholders always fall into one of three categories:

- Positive stakeholders – The people that are happy your project is happening and want the project to be successful.
- Negative stakeholders – The grumps/grouches that hate your project and hope that it (and maybe even you) go away and had never existed. In other words, they don't like your project.
- Neutral stakeholders – The individuals that are involved or affected by your project, but don't care if it succeeds or fails. Inspectors are good examples of neutral stakeholders.

2.2.1 Project Stakeholders

Common stakeholders
- Sponsor
- Customers and users
- Sellers
- Business partners
- Organizational groups
- Functional managers

Force Field Analysis

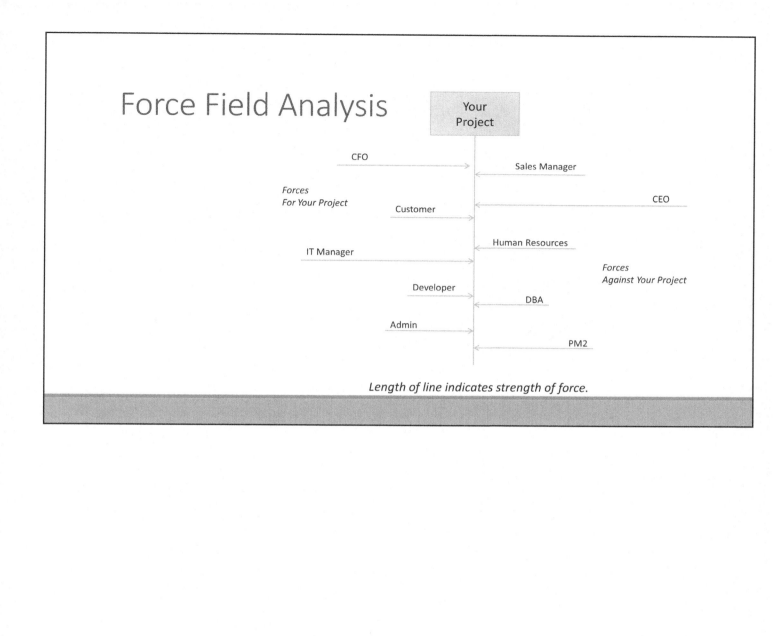

Length of line indicates strength of force.

2.2.2 Project Governance

Deliverable acceptance criteria

Escalation process

Relationship among projects, programs, project team, stakeholders

Process for communicating information

Decision-making process

Project life cycle approach

Process for stage gate or phase reviews

Control and oversight of the project

9.3.2.4 Establishing Ground Rules

Once the ground rules have been established, it's the responsibility of the entire project team to enforce the rules.

2.2.3 Project Success

Define what equates to project success first

Meeting project objectives

- Scope
- Costs
- Schedule
- Quality
- Resources
- Risk

2.3 Project Team

Dedicated – project team works on the project full time
- Collocated or virtual
- Reports directly to project manager
- Lines of authority are clear

Part-time – project team works part time on the project
- Carries on regular operational work
- Functional manager usually in control of project resources
- Project team could be on multiple projects at one time

PROJECT LIFE CYCLE

PROJECTS HAVE A UNIQUE LIFE CYCLE

Project stakeholders can be affected by the project life cycle. The project life cycle is unique to each project and is different from the project management life cycle. This lecture covers:

- Project stakeholders influence
- Project stakeholders and their contributions
- Project life cycle characteristics

_____

_____

_____

_____

_____

_____

_____

2.4 Project Life Cycle

Unique to each project

Duration of the project

Phases

Phases of construction versus phases of IT projects

| Concept | Design | Drawings | Bid | Construction |

A project life cycle is the progression of the project phases from the first phase all the way through the final project phase. Project life cycles are unique to application areas. You probably won't have too many foundation phases in health care or in IT. You would, of course, have phases that are logical to the application area you're working in – and that are unique to the project that you're managing.

2.4.2 Project Phases

Phases result in key deliverables

Phase names describe work:
- Foundation
- Framing
- Interior
- Exterior

Milestones often linked to phases

Phases can be called lots of things. Some organizations call phases stages. Other companies call phases a work unit. And your company may have an entirely different set of nomenclature for phases like just the name of the work that's happening in that phase. It's not big deal what terminology you want to assign to a phase – it's the concept that's important. A phase is a portion of the project that creates a deliverable and allows the next phase to begin.

Time and Influence

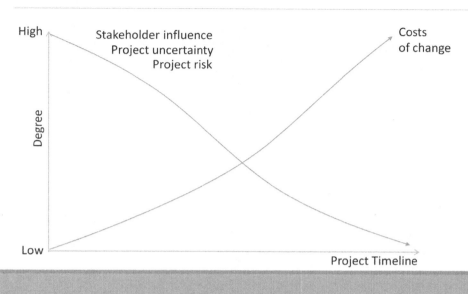

Degree: High — Low

Stakeholder influence
Project uncertainty
Project risk

Costs of change

Project Timeline

2.4 Product and Project Life Cycles

Life of the product

Last product phase is its retirement

Project life cycle typically does one of these activities (MACD):
- Moving
- Adding
- Changing
- Deleting

2.4.2.1 Project Phase Relationships

Sequential relationship

Overlapping relationship

Iterative relationship

"Love yourself first and everything else falls into line. You really have to love yourself to get anything done in this world."

– Lucille Ball

2.4.2.2 Predictive Life Cycles

Plan-driven

Waterfall approach

Predicts the project life cycle

Changes to scope are tightly controlled

2.4.2.3 Iterative and Incremental Life Cycles

Phases repeat through iterations

Iterations create deliverables

Detailed scope is elaborated for each iteration

Changes to the project scope are expected

2.4.2.4 Adaptive Life Cycles

Change-driven

Agile project management

Rapid iterations or project work

Backlog of requirements

Changes to the project scope are expected

_____

_____

_____

_____

_____

_____

_____

Learning Game!

http://www.instructing.com/wp-content/pub/2/story.html

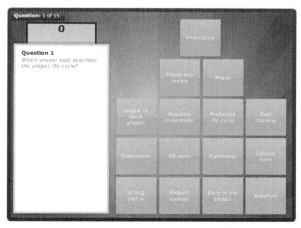

Chapter exam

_____

_____

_____

_____

_____

_____

_____

EXPLORE PROJECT MANAGEMENT PROCESSES

47 PROJECT MANAGEMENT PROCESSES

There are 47 project management processes that a project manager and the project team use to move a project along. The goal of these processes is to have a successful project, but a project's success is based on more than just leveraging these processes. A successful project depends on five things:

- Using the appropriate processes at the appropriate times
- Following a defined project management approach for execution and project control
- Developing and implementing a solid project management plan that addresses all areas of the project
- Conforming the project and the project management approach to the customer requirements
- Balancing the project time, cost, scope, quality, resources, and risks while meeting the project objectives

---

Project and Product Processes

Project management processes – flow of the project

Product processes – specify and create the project's product
- Vary by application area
- Execution of the project work
- Project scope defines the product
  - Construction
  - Computer programming
  - Network Infrastructure
  - Designing a web site

Project Management Processes

What is a process?
- Set of interrelated actions and activities
- Create a pre-specified result

Five groups of processes

47 project management processes

Inputs, Tools and Techniques, Outputs

Project Success Depends on...

 Use the most appropriate processes

 Use a defined and documented approach

 Comply with stakeholder requirements

 Balance time, cost, scope, quality, and risk

3.1 Project Management Processes

Apply globally across industries

You should not apply every process

Use the most appropriate processes

Depth of execution for each process used

_____

_____

_____

_____

_____

_____

_____

_____

Project Management Process Groups

Initiating – 13% of PMP exam questions

Planning – 24% of PMP exam questions

Executing – 31% of PMP exam questions

Monitoring and Controlling – 25% of PMP exam questions

Closing – 7% of PMP exam questions

WALK-THROUGH INITIATING PROCESSES

THERE ARE 2 INITIATING PROCESSES.

The project manager is assigned during initiation, and the inputs from the original project initiator and/or the project sponsor are considered throughout the initiation processes. Project initiation is, of course, the first process that kicks off the project. This exam-essential information includes:

- Getting the project initiated
- Developing the project charter
- Identifying the project stakeholders

3.3 Initiating Process Group

Two processes:
- Develop project charter
- Identify stakeholders

13% of PMP exam questions
26 questions

ANALYZE PLANNING PROCESSES

THERE ARE 24 PLANNING PROCESSES.

Projects fail at the beginning and not the end. A project needs effective planning, or it will be doomed. The whole point of the planning process group is to develop the project management plan. The good news is that the entire project plan doesn't have to happen in one session; in fact, planning is an iterative process, and the project manager and the project team return to the planning phase as needed to allow the project to move forward. Planning is key to project, and PMP, success. This lecture introduces:

Developing the project management plan
Planning the project scope
Collecting project requirements
Defining the project scope
Creating the Work Breakdown Structure
Planning for schedule management
Defining the project activities
Sequencing the project activities
Estimating the activity resources
Estimating the activity duration
Developing the project schedule
Planning project cost management

Estimating the project costs
Planning the project budget
Planning for quality
Completing human resources planning
Planning for project communications
Planning the project risks
Identifying the project risks
Performing qualitative risk analysis
Performing quantitative risk analysis
Planning for risk responses
Planning procurement management
Planning stakeholder management

3.4 Planning Process Group

24 processes:
- Develop project management plan
- Plan scope management
- Collect requirements
- Define scope
- Create work breakdown structure
- Plan schedule management
- Define activities

24% of PMP exam questions
48 questions

3.4 Planning Process Group

24 processes, continued:
- Sequence activities
- Estimate activity resources
- Estimate activity durations
- Develop schedule
- Plan cost management
- Estimate costs
- Determine budget

24% of PMP exam questions
48 questions

3.4 Planning Process Group

24 processes, continued:
- Plan quality management
- Plan human resource management
- Plan communications
- Plan risk management
- Identify risks
- Perform qualitative analysis
- Perform quantitative analysis

24% of PMP exam questions
48 questions

3.4 Planning Process Group

24 processes, continued:
- Plan risk responses
- Plan procurement management
- Plan stakeholder management

24% of PMP exam questions
48 questions

SURVEY
EXECUTING PROCESSES

THERE ARE 8 EXECUTING PROCESSES.

The executing processes allow the project work to be performed. They include the execution of the project plan, the execution of vendor management, and the management of the project implementation. The project manager works closely with the project team in this process group to ensure that the work is being completed and that the work results are of quality. The project manager also works with vendors to ensure that their procured work is complete, of quality, and meets the obligations of the contracts. The executing processes are all about getting the project work done. This lecture covers:

- Directing and managing project execution
- Performing quality assurance
- Acquiring the project team
- Developing the project team
- Managing the project team
- Managing project communications
- Conducting project procurements
- Managing stakeholder engagement

3.5 Executing Process Group

Eight processes
- Direct and manage project work
- Quality assurance
- Acquire project team
- Develop project team
- Manage project team
- Manage communications
- Conduct procurement
- Manage stakeholder engagement

31% of PMP exam questions
62 questions

REVIEW MONITORING AND CONTROLLING PROCESSES

THERE ARE 11 MONITORING AND CONTROLLING PROCESSES.

This process group focuses on monitoring the project work for variances, changes, and discrepancies so that corrective action can be used to ensure that the project continues to move toward its successful completion. This means lots of measuring, inspecting, and communicating with the project team to ensure that the project plan is followed, variances to the plan are reported, and responses can be expedited. While the project team does the work the project manager monitors and controls the work. This lecture details:

- Monitoring and controlling the project work
- Managing integrated change control
- Validating the project scope
- Controlling the project scope
- Controlling the project schedule
- Controlling the project costs
- Performing quality control
- Controlling communications
- Monitoring and controlling project risk
- Controlling project procurements
- Controlling stakeholder engagements

3.6 Monitoring and Controlling Process Group

11 processes
- Monitor and control project work
- Integrated change control
- Validate scope
- Control scope
- Control schedule

25% of PMP exam questions
50 questions

3.6 Monitoring and Controlling Process Group

11 processes, continued

- Control costs
- Control quality
- Control communications
- Control risks
- Control procurements
- Control stakeholder engagement

25% of PMP exam questions
50 questions

"The successful man is the one who finds out what is the matter with his business before his competitors do."

– Roy L. Smith

COMPLETE CLOSING PROCESSES

THERE ARE 2 CLOSING PROCESSES.

This process group focuses on monitoring the project work for variances, changes, and discrepancies so that corrective action can be used to ensure that the project continues to move toward its successful completion. This means lots of measuring, inspecting, and communicating with the project team to ensure that the project plan is followed, variances to the plan are reported, and responses can be expedited. Closing process include:

- Closing the project
- Closing procurement

3.7 Closing Process Group

Two processes
- Close project or phase
- Close procurement

7% of PMP exam questions
14 questions

WORK WITH PROJECT PROCESSES

PROJECT EVENTS DETERMINE WHICH PROCESS TO UTILIZE

3.8 Project Information

Work performance data – raw observation and measurements
- Percent of work completed
- Actual start and finish dates for activities
- Number of change requests, defects, actual costs

Work performance information – data that has been analyzed
- Status of deliverables
- Implementation status for change requests
- Forecasts for estimate to complete

Work performance reports – reports that communicate the work performance information

_____

_____

_____

_____

_____

_____

_____

3.9 Role of the Knowledge Areas

Ten project management knowledge areas:
- Project integration management
- Project scope management
- Project cost management
- Project schedule management
- Project quality management
- Project human resource management
- Project communications management
- Project risk management
- Project procurement management
- Project stakeholder management

Learning Game!

http://www.instructing.com/wp-content/pub/3/story.html

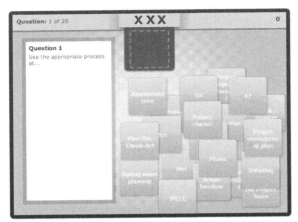

Chapter exam

MASTER PROJECT INTEGRATION MANAGEMENT

Choosing a Project

Opportunities

Problems

Customer request

Preparing to create the charter is often trickier than actually writing it. However, before the project management team can actually create a charter, there needs to be a project. This means the organization, the project steering committee, or the project portfolio management team needs to choose a project to initiate. There are reasons why some projects are selected and others are not. This lecture will explore:

- Why projects are selected by organizations
- Benefit measurement methods for project selection
- Time value of money
- Introduction to constrained optimization selection methods

_____

_____

_____

_____

_____

_____

_____

Benefits Measurement

Compare the benefits of the project

Cost-benefits ratio

Scoring models

Murder boards

Payback period

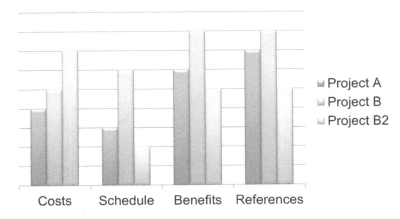

Project A
Project B
Project B2

Costs   Schedule   Benefits   References

Future Value of Money

FV=PV(1+i)n where:
- FV is future value
- PV is present value
- i is the given interest rate
- n is the number of time periods

Activity: Mary says her project needs $650,500 to complete and the project will last three years. If the rate of return is six percent what's the future value of Mary's project?

_____

_____

_____

_____

_____

_____

_____

Future Value of Money

FV=PV(1+i)n

- PV is $100,000
- i is .06
- n is five years

Future Value of Money

FV=PV$(1+i)n$

- PV is $100,000
- i is .06
- n is five years

FV=100,000$(1.06)5$

- FV=100,000(1.338226)
- FV=133,822.60

Present Value of Money

PV=FV/(1+i)n

- PV is present value
- FV is future value
- i is the given interest rate
- n is the number of time periods

Activity: Thomas promises that his project will be worth $1,500,000 in four years. If the rate of return is six percent what's the present value of this project?

_____

_____

_____

_____

_____

_____

_____

Present Value of Money

PV=FV/(1+i)n

- ○ FV is $160,000
- ○ i is .06
- ○ n is five years

PV=160,000/(1.338226)

PV=$119,561

_____

_____

_____

_____

_____

_____

_____

Net Present Value

Finds the true value of a project

Considers a project with multiple returns

Considers the initial cash outlay

While future value and present value do show the time value of money they both have one distinct disadvantage: they don't account for monies earned while the project is in motion. While many projects, like construction for example, don't realize a return on investment until the project is completed, other projects, like IT, retail, and healthcare, realize return on investment in phases.

Net Present Value

Calculate the return for each time period

Calculate each time period's present value

Sum the present value

Subtract the investment

NPV greater than zero is good

Net Present Value

Time Period	Cash Flow	Present Value
1	$15,000	$14,150.94
2	$25,000	$22,249.91
3	$17,000	$14,273.53
4	$25,000	$19,802.34
5	$18,000	$13,450.65
Totals	$100,000	$83,927.37
Investments		$78,000.00
Net Present Value		$5,927.37

Internal Rate of Return

Present value equals cash inflow

IRR with higher values are good

IRR with lower values might be poor

LAUNCH A NEW PROJECT

EXAMINING THE DOCUMENTS FOR NEW PROJECTS

The project charter, as a final reminder for your exam, is endorsed by an entity outside of the project boundaries. This person or entity has the power to authorize the project and grant the project manager the power to assign resources to the project work. The project charter should define the business needs and what the project aims to create in order to solve those business needs. You'll need to know how project charters are written. This includes:

- Project statement of work
- Business cases
- Using expert judgment
- Identifying the contents of the project charter

4.1 Develop Project Charter

Authorized external to the project

Appropriate power

Portfolio Steering Committee

The project charter authorizes the project. This document launches the project and gives the project manager the authority to use organizational monies and resources to reach the objectives of the project. It's a powerful document, and without one of these you're setting yourself (and often your project) up for failure.

_____

_____

_____

_____

_____

_____

_____

ITTO: Develop Project Charter

Inputs	Tools & Techniques	Outputs
Project statement of work	Expert judgment	Project charter
Business case	Facilitation techniques	
Agreements		
Enterprise environmental factors		
Organizational process assets		

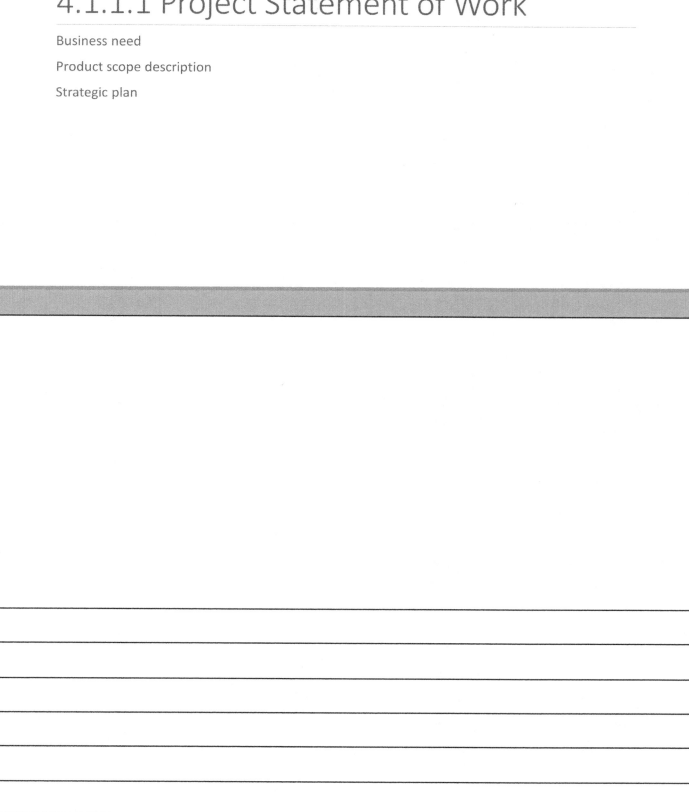

4.1.1.1 Project Statement of Work

Business need

Product scope description

Strategic plan

4.1.1.2 Examining the Business Case

Determines worth of the project

Justifies the investment

Created as a result of:
- Market demand
- Organizational need
- Customer request
- Technological advance
- Legal requirement
- Ecological impacts
- Social need

_____

_____

_____

_____

_____

_____

_____

4.1.2 Creating the Project Charter

Expert judgment
- Consultants
- Internal organizational resources
- Stakeholders
- Industry groups
- PMO

Facilitation techniques
- Brainstorming
- Conflict resolution
- Meeting management

Developing the Project Charter

Requirements for satisfaction

Approval requirements

Project manager

Project sponsor

High-level purpose of the project

Developing the Project Charter

Purpose of the project

Milestone schedule

Stakeholder influence

Risks

Developing the Project Charter

Functional organizations

Summary budget

Contract

PLAN THE PROJECT

PLANNING IS AN ITERATIVE ACTIVITY THROUGHOUT THE PROJECT.

One of my favorite project management axioms is that projects fail at the beginning not the end. Show me a project management team that doesn't take time to plan, and I'll show you a project management team that struggles to finish their projects on time, on scope, and on budget. It's not much fun for anyone involved in the project when projects crash and burn due to avoidable mistakes. Planning is paramount.

ITTO: Develop Project Management Plan

Inputs	Tools & Techniques	Outputs
Project charter	Expert judgment	Project management plan
Outputs from other processes	Facilitation techniques	
Enterprise environmental factors		
Organizational process assets		

"You have to learn the rules of the game. And then you have to play better than anyone else."

— Albert Einstein

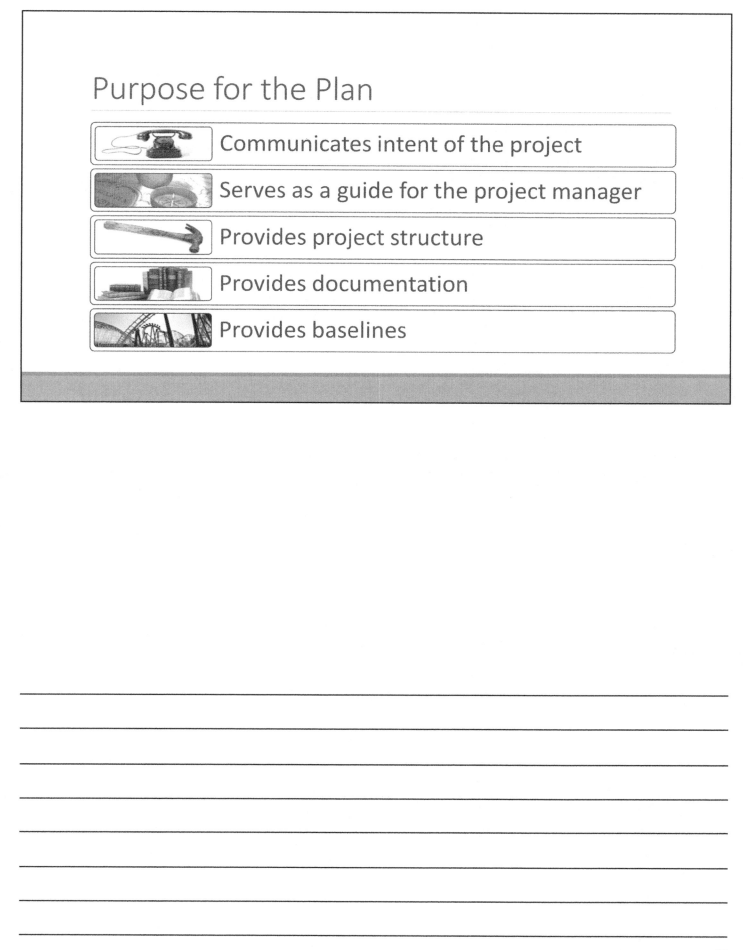

Purpose for the Plan

- Communicates intent of the project
- Serves as a guide for the project manager
- Provides project structure
- Provides documentation
- Provides baselines

Developing the Project Plan

Triple Constraints of Project Management

Iron Triangle

Balance time, cost, and scope constraints

So when does a project manager and the project team do planning? In theory planning comes right after initiating and before executing. In reality, planning overlaps initiating just a bit and extends deep into the project's execution. Planning is full of iterative processes that demand the project manager and the project team to revisit them early and often. Planning ends when the project work is done and the final project process group – closing – begins.

Planning Participants

Participant	Contribution
Project manager	Leadership, facilitation, organization, direction, expert judgment
Project team members	Knowledge of project work, time estimating, schedule, risk assessment, expert judgment
Customers	Objectives, quality requirements, influence on budget and schedule
Management	Budget, resources, project management methodology, quality requirements, project plan approval

Typical Project Management Plan

Change management plan

Communications management plan

Configuration management plan

Cost baseline

Cost management plan

HR management plan

Process improvement plan

Procurement management plan

Scope baseline

Quality management plan

Requirements management plan

Risk management plan

Schedule baseline

Schedule management plan

Scope management plan

Stakeholder management plan

Activity attributes	Activity cost estimates	Activity duration estimates	Activity list
Activity resource requirements	Agreements	Basis of estimates	Change log
Change requests	Forecasts (costs, schedule)	Procurement documents	Procurement statement of work
Issue log	Milestone list	Project funding requirements	Project schedule
Project calendars	Project charter	Project statement of work	Quality checklists
Project schedule network diagrams	Project staff assignments	Requirements documentation	Requirements traceability matrix
Quality control measurements	Quality metrics	Risk register	Schedule data
Resource breakdown structure	Resource calendars	Stakeholder register	Team performance assessments
Seller proposals	Source selection criteria	Work performance reports	Work performance data
Work performance information			

Here's a list of the typical project documents:

Activity attributes
Activity cost estimates
Activity duration estimates
Activity list
Activity resource requirements
Agreements
Basis of estimates
Change log
Change requests
Forecasts (costs, schedule)
Procurement documents
Procurement statement of work
Issue log
Milestone list
Project funding requirements
Project schedule
Project calendars
Project charter

Project statement of work
Quality checklists
Project schedule network diagrams
Project staff assignments
Requirements documentation
Requirements traceability matrix
Quality control measurements
Quality metrics
Risk register
Schedule data
Resource breakdown structure
Resource calendars
Stakeholder register
Team performance assessments
Seller proposals
Source selection criteria
Work performance reports
 Work performance data
Work performance information

EXECUTE THE PROJECT PLANS

PROJECT MANAGEMENT IS ABOUT GETTING THINGS DONE.

The product of the project is created during these execution processes. The largest percentage of the project budget will be spent during project execution. The project manager and the project team must work together to orchestrate the timing and integration of all the project's moving parts. A flaw in one area of the execution can have ramifications in cost and additional risk, and can cause additional flaws in other areas of the project. Once you have a plan you'll execute it. This lecture covers:

- Executing the project work
- Directing the project team
- Examining the project deliverables
- Applying project actions

4.3 Direct and Manage Project Work

Doing the work to satisfy the project objectives

Spending funds to satisfy the project objectives

Managing, training, and leading the project team

Completing procurement requirements

Managing sellers

Acquiring, managing, and using resources such as materials, tools, facilities, and equipment to get the project work completed

The project planning is iterative while the project execution – you hope – happens just once. In other words, you want the project work to be done correctly the first time. Executing the project is where the bulk of the project's time and monies are consumed. It's in this process group that you're spending the project budget on materials and labor.

4.3 Direct and Manage Project Work

Managing risks

Fleshing approved changes into the project

Managing communications

Collecting project data on schedules, costs, quality, and overall project progress—and then reporting on these components

Completing lessons learned documentation

Managing stakeholder engagement

ITTO: Direct and Manage Project Work

Inputs	Tools & Techniques	Outputs
Project management plan	Expert judgment	Deliverables
Approved change requests	Project management information system	Work performance data
Enterprise environmental factors	Meetings	Change requests
Organizational process assets		Project management plan updates
		Project documents updates

Actions in Execution

Corrective action – realigns project performance

Preventive action – ensures future performance

Defect repair – modifies nonconformance to project requirements

These actions usually require a change request

Corrective Actions

Fixing the project

Defect repair

Defect repair validation

Preventive Actions

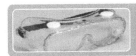 Safety

 Training

 Anticipated problems

 Risk management

MONITOR AND CONTROL THE PROJECT

MONITORING AND CONTROLLING HAPPENS IN TANDEM WITH PROJECT EXECUTION

As soon as a project begins, the project management monitoring and controlling processes also begin. These processes monitor all the other processes within the project to ensure they are being done according to plan, according to the performing organization's practices, and to ensure that a limited number of defects enters the project.

- Examining project performance
- Tracking and monitoring project risks
- Maintaining product information
- Forecasting the project's success
- Monitoring approved changes

_____

_____

_____

_____

_____

_____

_____

4.4 Monitor and Control Project Work

Compare actual experiences to project management plan

Assess project performance

Identify new risks

Maintain information about the project's current state

Wouldn't it be great if you and your project team could just create the project management plan, and then the project team would just go do the project work? You could spend your mornings sleeping in and your afternoons on the golf course. Of course, if that were the case there'd be no reasons to have a project manager. Projects, like most things in life, require a constant monitoring and controlling.

ITTO: Monitor and Control Project Work

Inputs	Tools & Techniques	Outputs
Project management plan	Expert judgment	Change requests
Schedule forecasts	Analytical techniques	Work performance reports
Cost forecasts	Project management information system	Project management plan updates
Validated changes	Meetings	Project documents updates
Work performance information		
Enterprise environmental factors		
Organizational process assets		

Enterprise Environmental Factors

Government and industry standards

Company work authorization system

Risk tolerances

PMIS

Organizational Process Assets

Communication requirements

Financial control procedures

Issue and defect management procedures

Change control procedures

Risk control procedures

Process measurement database

Lessons learned database

Forecasting Project Performance

Schedule forecasts
- Estimate to complete
- Schedule variance
- Schedule performance index

Costs forecasts
- Estimate to complete
- Estimate at completion
- Cost variance
- Cost performance index

PERFORM INTEGRATED CHANGE CONTROL

CHANGE CAN AFFECT THE ENTIRE PROJECT

Changes can affect all areas of the project. Consider a change in the project scope and how it could affect the project budget, schedule, quality, human resources, communications, risks, procurement and even other stakeholders.

- Using change control tools
- Examining integrated change control
- Applying configuration management

4.5 Perform Integrated Change Control

Ensure only approved changes

Review change requests promptly

Manage approved changes

Maintain baselines

Review, approve, or decline change requests

Coordinate changes across project

Document change request and impact

ITTO: Perform Integrated Change Control

Inputs	Tools & Techniques	Outputs
Project management plan	Expert judgment	Approved change requests
Work performance reports	Meetings	Change log
Change requests	Change control tools	Project management plan updates
Enterprise environmental factors		Project documents updates
Organizational process assets		

Configuration Control

Specification the deliverables and the processes

Features and functions

How the project work is completed

Configuration Control

Configuration identification – identification and documentation of the product and its components

Configuration status accounting – includes the documentation of the product information

Configuration verification and auditing – concerned with performance and functional attributes of the product

_____

_____

_____

_____

_____

_____

_____

_____

Managing Project Change

 Documented change requests

 Unapproved changes

 Scope creep

 Gold plating

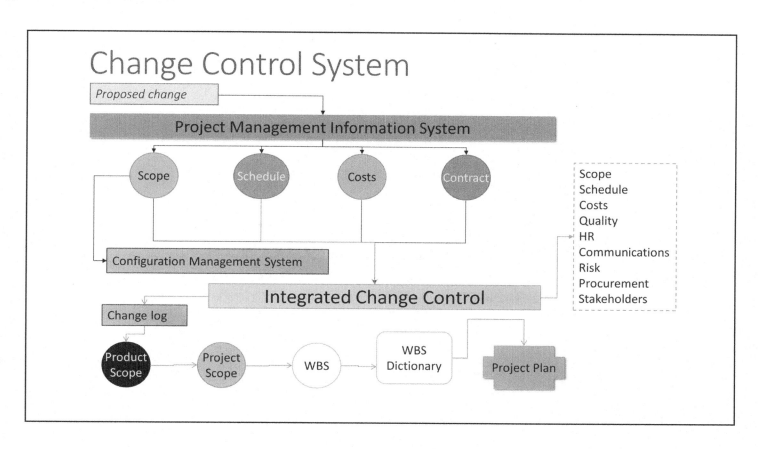

Change Control System

Every change that enters the project must pass through this change control process. If not – lookout! There's a good chance that problems are lurking just below the surface in that project. Examples include unchecked risks, cost overruns, missed deadlines, and frustrations from the project team, the project customers, and management. Trouble abounds.

CLOSE THE PROJECT

CLOSING IS THE HAPPIEST DAY OF THE PROJECT

Every project manager that I know loves to close a project. There's something rewarding about completing a project and then transferring the deliverable to the customer or project user. I've also learned from participant feedback in my PMP Exam Prep seminars that this topic is the category where exam candidates missed the most questions on their way to their PMP certification. I believe it's because folks have a tendency to study in the order of the process groups: initiation, planning, executing, monitoring and controlling, and then (finally) closing. I imagine they're winded by the time their studying efforts get to closing. With that in mind, really home in on this closing discussion. I want you to pass your exam!

- Performing administrative closure
- Closing the project contracts
- Closing the project
- Update the organizational process assets

4.6 Close Project or Phase

Contract documentation

Enterprise environmental factors

Work performance information

Deliverables

Preparing to archive

The two most exciting days in a project manager's life is when a project is first started and when it's ending. Okay, so that may be a slight exaggeration, but there really is something exciting about closing a project. You, the project manager, know that the work has been done with quality, the project customer is excited about the project deliverable, the project team is happy the project's done, and management is ready for you to move onto other assignments.

Sometimes closing the project isn't nearly as cheery a picture as I paint above. Sometimes the project is riddled with trouble, the project team is frustrated with the work, the project's over budget, late or worse yet, the project has been canceled altogether. Canceled projects shouldn't just be thrown out. The close project processes can offer some insight into what worked, what didn't, and what the project manager, the project team, and even management, should do better next time around.

ITTO: Close Project or Phase

Inputs	Tools & Techniques	Outputs
Project management plan	Expert judgment	Final product, service, or result transition
Accepted deliverables	Analytical techniques	Organizational process assets updates
Organizational process assets	Meetings	

Closing the Project

Assembling project records

Project success or failure

Lessons learned documentation

Archiving the records

Learning Game!

http://www.instructing.com/wp-content/pub/4/story.html

Chapter exam

PLAN PROJECT SCOPE MANAGEMENT

MANAGING ALL OF THE REQUIRED WORK – AND ONLY THE REQUIRED WORK

One of the first things you'll have to achieve in your role as the project manager of a new project is to define the project's scope management plan. Now, your organization may rely on organizational process assets in the form of a template for all projects, but it's possible that you'll be creating this scope management plan from scratch. In this section, you'll learn both approaches that you can apply to your projects and your PMI exam. This lecture includes:

- Relying on project information
- Using templates and forms
- Creating the Project Scope Management Plan
- Performing product analysis
- Using alternative identification
- Interviewing experts and stakeholders

5.1 Planning Scope Management

Creates the scope management plan to:
- Documents scope definition process
- Scope validation process
- Scope control process

Offer direction for scope management

Helps combat scope creep

ITTO: Planning Scope Management

Inputs	Tools & Techniques	Outputs
Project management plan	Expert judgment	Scope management plan
Project charter	Meetings	Requirements management plan
Enterprise environmental factors		
Organizational process assets		

Project and Product Scope

Product scope – features and functions

Project scope – work to be completed

Product Scope

Project Scope

Features and functions are key to developing the requirements of the product scope. These two words are attached to a commonly misused term in project management: configuration management. Configuration management is managing, documenting, and controlling the features and functions of the product as the product is being created within project management.

COLLECT PROJECT REQUIREMENTS

REQUIREMENTS ARE WHAT THE PROJECT MUST ADHERE TO AND DELIVER FOR THE PROJECT TO BE SUCCESSFUL

The second plan that comes out of scope planning is the requirements management plan. While similar in nature, this plan explains how the project will collect, analyze, record, and manage the requirements throughout the project. Like the scope management plan, this plan doesn't list the actual requirements, but sets the rules for how the project manager, team, and stakeholders will interact with the project's requirements. This plan is also a subsidiary plan for the overall project management plan. The project requirements are defined through many tools and techniques to help document the requirements and to create a requirements traceability matrix. This lecture details:

- Working with stakeholders to define requirements
- Requirement gathering techniques
- Documenting and publishing requirements
- Creating a requirements traceability matrix

5.2 Collect Requirements

Business requirements: higher-level needs of the organization

Stakeholder requirements: needs of a stakeholder or stakeholder group

Solution requirements: features, functions, and characteristics of the product, service
- Functional requirements describe the behaviors of the product.
- Nonfunctional requirements describe the environmental conditions or qualities

Transition requirements: moving from the current state to the future state.

Project requirements: actions, processes, or other conditions

Quality requirements: criteria needed to validate the successful completion of a project deliverable or fulfillment of other project requirements

ITTO: Collect Requirements

Inputs	Tools & Techniques	Outputs
Scope management plan	Interviews	Requirements documentation
Requirements management plan	Focus groups	Requirements traceability matrix
Stakeholder management plan	Facilitated workshops	
Project charter	Group creativity techniques	
Stakeholder register	Group decision-making techniques	
	Questionnaires and surveys	
	Observations	
	Prototypes	
	Benchmarking	
	Context diagrams	
	Document analysis	

Interviewing Stakeholders

Stakeholder register

One-to-one

One-to-many

Many-to-many

Focus Groups

Moderated event

6-12 people

Neutral moderator

Participant composition

Facilitated Workshop

Requirements workshop

Commonality, consensus, cohesion

Joint application design workshop

Voice of the customer

Quality function deployment

"I attribute my success to this: I never gave or took any excuse."

— Florence Nightingale

Group Creativity Techniques

Brainstorming

Nominal group technique

Mind mapping

Affinity diagram

Delphi Techniques

| Survey One Broad | Survey Two More specific | Survey Three | Survey Four | *Delphi technique* |

Using Group Decisions

Unanimity – everyone agrees

Majority – more than 50 percent agrees

Plurality – largest block agrees

Dictatorship – power decides

_____

_____

_____

_____

_____

_____

_____

_____

Questionnaires and Surveys

Large group

Paper-based

Web-based

Geographical concerns

Stakeholder Observation

Job shadowing

Passive

Active (participant observer)

Prototypes

Throw-away prototypes

Functional prototypes

Storyboarding

Benchmarking the Requirements

Comparing two or more system, businesses, approaches

Set an external basis for performance

Comparing organizations for requirements

Utilizing a Context Diagram

Scope model

Business system working components
- Servers
- Workstations
- Databases
- Workflow
- People (actors)

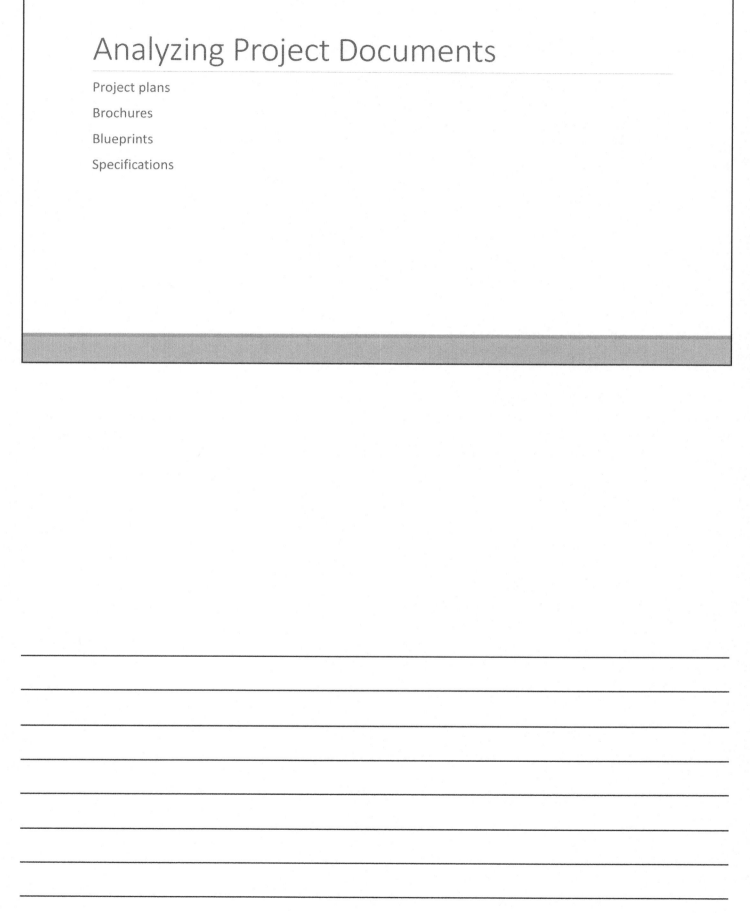

Analyzing Project Documents

Project plans

Brochures

Blueprints

Specifications

Managing the Project Requirements

Requirements Traceability Matrix
- Table of requirements
- Business needs
- Project objectives
- WBS deliverables
- Product components
- Development
- Related test cases

Objectives are the goals of the project – the measurable, quantifiable goals of the project. Think of time, cost, quality, technical requirements, blueprints, and product acceptance criteria. I stress the word quantifiable – avoid loose terms in your objectives such as fast, good, satisfaction, and other subjective terms. What's fast to you may be slow to your customer. If you can attach a metric you need to.

DEFINE THE PROJECT SCOPE

THE PROJECT SCOPE STATEMENT DEFINES THE OBJECTIVES OF THE PROJECT ENDEAVOR

The project scope statement is one of the most important documents in the project. This lecture covers:
- Detailing the project objectives
- Describing the product scope
- Defining the project requirements
- Establishing the project boundaries
- Defining the project acceptance criteria
- Identifying the project constraints
- Listing the project assumptions
- Defining the initial project organization
- Defining the initial project risks
- Determining the schedule milestones
- Setting fund limitations
- Estimating the project costs
- Determining the project configuration management requirements
- Identifying project specification documents
- Documenting the project approval requirements

5.3 Define Scope

Detailed description the project and the product

Project boundaries

Project scope statement

Scope baseline
- Project scope statement
- Project WBS
- Project WBS dictionary

ITTO: Define Scope

Inputs	Tools & Techniques	Outputs
Scope management plan	Expert judgment	Project scope statement
Project charter	Product analysis	Project documents updates
Requirements documentation	Alternatives generation	
Organizational process assets	Facilitated workshops	

Defining the Project Scope

Expert judgment
- Consultants
- Stakeholders, including customers
- Professional and technical associations
- Industry groups
- Subject matter experts

The project scope statement is a document that defines what the project is, the project deliverables, and the work that the project team (and likely contractors) will have to do in order to create the identified project deliverables. The major purpose of the document is to communicate with the project team, the project customers, and the project stakeholders a common understanding of the project's purpose, goals, and objectives. The project scope statement, as I'll dive into one moment, also serves as a launching board for additional planning by the project team and the project manager.

Product Analysis

Product breakdown

Systems engineering

Value engineering

Value analysis

Function analysis

Quality function deployment

Remember the phrase "features and functions" and the product scope? This section of the project scope statement defines the level of control the project manager (and, often by proxy, the organization) will place over the project change control requirements. Changes to the product scope will result in changes to the project scope.

_____

_____

_____

_____

_____

_____

_____

Alternatives Generation

Benchmarking

Systems

Vendors

Materials

Resources

Alternative identification, just like it sounds, is a method to identify any other solutions, approaches, or deliverables that would satisfy the customer's product scope. For example, a customer wants an email server. They don't care if you use Microsoft Exchange Server or some home-grown POP3 mail server. All they want is an email server that allows their staff to send and receive email. Alternative identification would identify, compare, and contrast all the available solutions for the customer.

_____

_____

_____

_____

_____

_____

_____

Facilitated Workshops

Stakeholder expectations

Documentation

Communication

Verification

Business analysts

Examining a Project Scope Statement

Product scope description

Product acceptance criteria

Project deliverables

Project exclusions

Project constraints

Project assumptions

Project Charter versus Project Scope

Project Charter
- Project purpose or justification
- Measurable project objectives
- High-level requirements
- High-level project description
- High-level risks
- Summary milestone schedule
- Summary budget
- Stakeholder list
- Project approval requirements
- Assigned project manager, responsibility, and authority level
- Name and authority of the sponsor

Project Scope
- Project scope description
- Acceptance criteria
- Project deliverables
- Project exclusions
- Project constraints
- Project assumptions

Project Scope Statement Updated Docs

Stakeholder register

Requirements documentation

Requirements traceability matrix

CREATE THE WBS

THE WORK BREAKDOWN STRUCTURE IS A DECOMPOSITION OF THE PROJECT SCOPE

A key concept for your PMP exam, and often your projects, is the Work Breakdown Structure (WBS). The WBS is all about the project deliverables. It's a breakdown of the project scope into hierarchical deliverables. The WBS takes the project scope and breaks it down into smaller, manageable chunks of deliverables. Each layer of the WBS breaks down the layer above it into smaller deliverables, until it arrives at the smallest item in the WBS, the work package. This lecture details:

- Defining the WBS
- Using a WBS template
- Decomposing the project scope
- Creating the WBS
- Creating the WBS dictionary
- Defining the scope baseline

5.4 Create WBS

Process of decomposing the project scope

Deliverables-orientated

Not the activities list

Major component of the scope baseline

Project planning tools

Visualizes the project

Defines what's in scope

Deterrent to scope change

ITTO: Create WBS

Inputs	Tools & Techniques	Outputs
Scope management plan	Decomposition	Scope baseline
Project scope statement	Expert judgment	Project documents updates
Requirements documentation		
Enterprise environmental factors		
Organizational process assets		

WBS Creation

Major project deliverables identified

Structure and organize the WBS

Decompose upper-level components to lower-level components

Assigning identification codes to components

Verify the scope decomposition

The WBS is a decomposition of the project scope statement. It is a deliverables-oriented document that visualizes all the things the project will create. It is not, and I stress the word not, the activity list. The WBS takes the project scope statement and breaks it down into the deliverables the customer is expecting from the project. It organizes and catalogs the project deliverables.

_____

_____

_____

_____

_____

_____

_____

Finalizing the WBS

Control accounts for work packages

Code of accounts - unique identifier

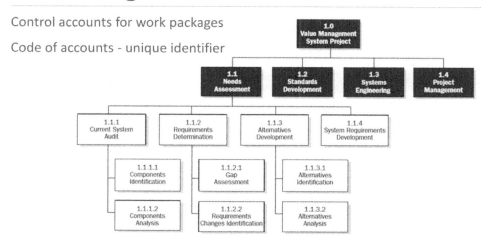

WBS Templates

Historical information

Pre-populated deliverables

Sometimes called a WBT

Just as each project scope statement is unique, so too must each WBS be unique. Having said that, it is acceptable to use a WBS from a previous, similar project and adapt it to your current project as a WBS template. Some organizations have a consistent level of deliverables with all of their projects so they use a pre-populated template to reflect these "every project" deliverables. For example, you might create a template that reflects your project management plans, quality control charts, and expected reports that the project will generate.

WBS Dictionary

Defines all elements of the WBS

Defines work package attributes

Time, cost, requirements, resources

Follows WBS usage

WBS Dictionary includes:

- Code of account identifier
- Description of work
- Assumptions and constraints
- Responsible organization
- List of schedule milestone
- Associated schedule activities
- Resources required
- Cost estimates
- Quality requirements
- Acceptance criteria
- Technical references
- Contract information

Scope Baseline

Project scope statement

WBS

WBS Dictionary

VALIDATE PROJECT SCOPE

SCOPE VALIDATION LEADS TO CUSTOMER ACCEPTANCE OF THE PROJECT WORK

Scope validation is the process of the project customer accepting the project deliverables. It happens either at the end of each project phase or as major deliverables are created. Scope validation ensures that the deliverables the project creates are in alignment with the project scope. It is concerned with the acceptance of the work. A related activity, quality control (QC), is concerned with the correctness of the work. Poor quality will typically result in scope validation failure. How do you know your scope and deliverables are valid? This lecture will help you to understand:

- Defining scope validation
- Performing scope validation
- Group-decision making techniques
- Gaining project acceptance

5.5 Validate Scope

Inspection-driven process

Customer inspects the project work

Phase and project completion

Review, audits, walkthroughs

Leads to formal project acceptance

ITTO: Validate Scope

Inputs	Tools & Techniques	Outputs
Project management plan	Inspection	Accepted deliverables
Requirements documentation	Group decision-making techniques	Change requests
Requirements traceability matrix		Work performance information
Verified deliverables		Project documents updates.
Work performance data		

Inspecting the Project Work

Measuring

Examining

Testing

Validating

Reviews

Walk-throughs

Audits

Scope validation is an inspection-driven process that the project customer completes. Scope validation is a formal sign-off on the work that has been completed so far in the project, and it allows the project to move onto the next project phase. In a larger project the completion of a phase constitutes a phased gate which allows the project to move onto the next project phase – and to be funded to reach the next phase of the project.

_____

_____

_____

_____

_____

_____

_____

Formally Accepting the Project Work

Accepted deliverables for phases and the project

Sign-off of deliverables

Change requests are a possible output

Scope verification and quality control

"Doing the best at this moment puts you in the best place for the next moment."

– Oprah Winfrey

CONTROL THE PROJECT SCOPE

YOU MUST CONTROL THE PROJECT SCOPE TO ENSURE THAT YOU'RE DELIVERING EXACTLY WHAT THE CUSTOMER HAS REQUESTED

Scope control is about protecting the project scope from change and, when change does happen, managing those changes. Ideally, all requested changes follow the scope change control system, which means that change requests must be documented. Those changes that sneak into the project scope are lumped into that project poison category of scope creep. Scope creep is, of course, bad, bad news. You must protect the project scope from changes and this lecture will help. You'll learn:

- Establishing a change control system
- Studying variances
- Replanning the project work
- Revisiting the configuration management system

5.6 Control Scope

Are changes agreed upon?

Has the change already happened?

How to manage the existing change?

How to incorporate approved changes?

What baselines are affected by the change?

ITTO: Control Scope

Inputs	Tools & Techniques	Outputs
Project management plan	Variance analysis	Work performance information
Requirements documentation		Change requests
Requirements traceability matrix		Project management plan updates
Work performance data		Project documents updates
Organizational process assets		Organizational process assets updates

Variance Analysis

Performance measurements

Magnitude of variation

Determine cause and degree of variance

Corrective or preventive action

Updating the Scope Statement

Change affects the project scope statement

Versioning is appropriate

Approved changes affect the scope baseline

Could affect cost and schedule baselines

Learning Game!

http://www.instructing.com/wp-content/pub/5/story.html

Chapter exam

PLAN SCHEDULE MANAGEMENT

PLANNING, ESTIMATING, SCHEDULING, AND CONTROLLING THE PROJECT WORK TO FINISH ON TIME

The project management planning processes are iterative, as you know, and will happen over and over throughout the project. You and the project team—and even some key stakeholders—will work together to define the project's schedule management plan. This will happen early in the project's planning processes, but chances are good you'll need to return to schedule management planning to adjust, replan, or focus on the schedule you've created for the project. Schedules are created and designed throughout the project. This lecture will help you to understand these concepts:

- Examining policies and procedures
- Working with a deadline
- Creating the schedule based on scope

6.1 Plan Schedule Management

Defines how the schedule will be:
- Developed
- Managed
- Executed
- Controlled

Defines schedule management approach for entire project

ITTO: Plan Schedule Management

Inputs	Tools & Techniques	Outputs
Project management plan	Expert judgment	Schedule management plan
Project charter	Analytical techniques	
Enterprise environmental factors	Meetings	
Organizational process assets		

What's in the Schedule Management Plan?

Schedule management plan includes:
- Project schedule model development
- Level of accuracy
- Units of measure (hours, days, weeks)
- Organizational procedure links
- Project schedule model maintenance
- Control thresholds
- Rules for performance measurements
- Reporting formats
- Process descriptions

This subsidiary plan details how the project schedule will be managed, monitored and controlled, and protected from change. It will identify the project phases, milestones, and circumstances which could affect the project's schedule, such as vendor delays, outside resources, or dependence on the outputs of other projects.

_____

_____

_____

_____

_____

_____

_____

DEFINE THE PROJECT ACTIVITIES

ACTIVITIES CREATE THE ELEMENTS WITHIN THE PROJECT'S WORK BREAKDOWN STRUCTURE

When a project is first initiated, project managers often focus immediately on the labor and activities that will be required to complete the project work. But that focus ignores the scope. In Chapter 5, I discussed the project scope and the work breakdown structure (WBS) as prerequisites to defining the project activities. Before the work actually begins you'll need to work with the project team to define the activities to schedule. This lecture covers:

- Examining the inputs to activity definition
- Decomposing the project work
- Relying on project templates
- Using rolling wave planning
- Planning for more work
- Examining the project activities and their attributes

6.2 Define Activities

Activities associated with work packages

Basis for estimating, scheduling, and controlling work

Activities list

Activity attributes

Milestone list

ITTO: Define Activities

Inputs	Tools & Techniques	Outputs
Schedule management plan	Decomposition	Activity list
Scope baseline	Rolling wave planning	Activity attributes
Enterprise environmental factors	Expert judgment	Milestone list
Organizational process assets		

Defining the Project Activities

Project work and project manager work

Planning processes

Sequence of activities

Procurement time

Internal and external events

Known and unknown events

Decomposing Project Activities

Activity list and work packages

8/80 Rule

Requires three inputs:
- Scope baseline
- Enterprise environmental factors
- Organizational process assets

_____

_____

_____

_____

_____

_____

_____

_____

Activity List

Separate document

Lists all project activities

Activity identifier

Scope of work description

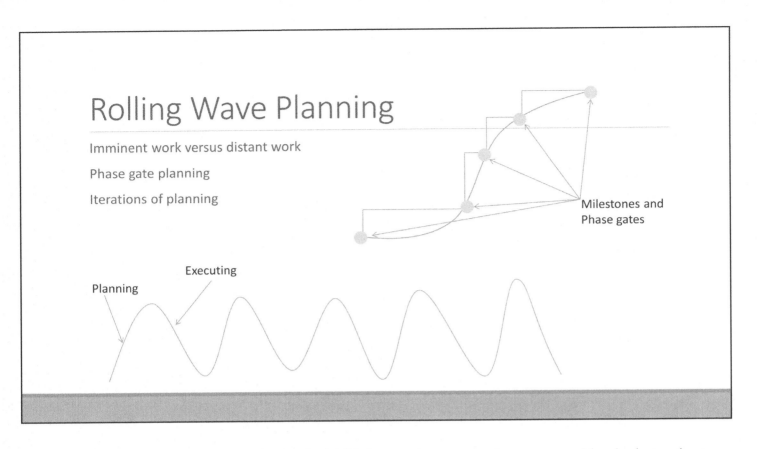

So what's a phased-gate estimate? Glad you asked. This is an estimate type where you provide a budget estimate for the entire project, as in $80 million, but then you prepare a very detailed phased-gate estimate for the phase that's about to begin. This estimate is very detailed and shows management and the stakeholders what they're getting for their money during this project phase. In our $80 million project a phased-gate estimate for the current phase may be five million. The monies spent in each phase totals $80 million.

Templates

Historical information

Pre-populated forms and plans

Organizational process assets

Planning Components

Control accounts
- Management control point
- Scope, cost, and schedule
- Performance measurement

Planning packages
- Decisions to be completed
- Issues

Activity Attributes

Activity name and description

Activity ID

WBS identifier

Relationships

Leads and lags

Activity Attributes

Resource requirements

Imposed dates

Constraints and assumptions

Additional information

SEQUENCE THE PROJECT ACTIVITIES

SEQUENCE THE ACTIVITIES IN THE BEST ORDER TO REACH THE END OF THE PROJECT

Now that the activity list has been created, the activities must be arranged in a logical sequence. This process calls on the project manager and the project team to identify the logical relationships between activities, as well as the preferred relationship between those activities. Once you have the activities defined you'll need to put them in the correct order. That's what this module is all about:

- Defining the activity relationships
- Determining the network structure to use
- Establishing activity dependencies
- Applying leads and lags

6.3 Sequence Activities

Computer-driven

Manual process

Blended approach

Predecessors and successors

Milestone list

ITTO: Sequence Activities

Inputs	Tools & Techniques	Outputs
Schedule management plan	Precedence diagramming method (PDM)	Project schedule network diagrams
Activity list	Dependency determination	Project documents updates
Activity attributes	Leads and lags	
Milestone list		
Project scope statement		
Enterprise environmental factors		
Organizational process assets		

Precedence Diagramming Method

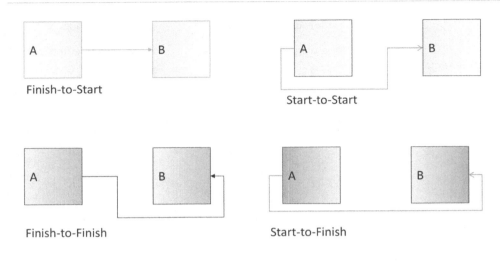

1. **Finish-to-start:** Activity A must finish before Activity B can start. Example: The walls must be primed before the walls can be painted. This is the most common relationship you'll use in project management.
2. **Start-to-start:** Activity C must start before Activity D can start. You'll use this relationship type when you want two activities to both start at the same time. Example: The network cable installation activity must start so that the network patch panel can be installed. Both activities can happen at the same time.
3. **Finish-to-finish:** Activity E must finish so that Activity F can finish. You'll use this relationship type when you want, surprise, surprise, both activities to finish at approximately the same time. Example: The software installation activity must finish so the software training class can finish. Users in the software training class will return to their desktops to find the software they've just been trained on is now installed on their computer.
4. **Start-to-Finish:** Activity H must start so that Activity G can finish. This is the most unusual and least used relationship type. This relationship is primarily used with just-in-time manufacturing, just-in-time scheduling, and inventory management systems.

Dependency Determination

Mandatory dependencies – hard logic

Discretionary dependencies – soft logic

External dependencies – external constraint

Internal dependencies – type of hard logic

Leads and Lags

Lead is accelerated time

Lead allows activities to overlap

Lag is waiting time

Lag moves activities farther apart

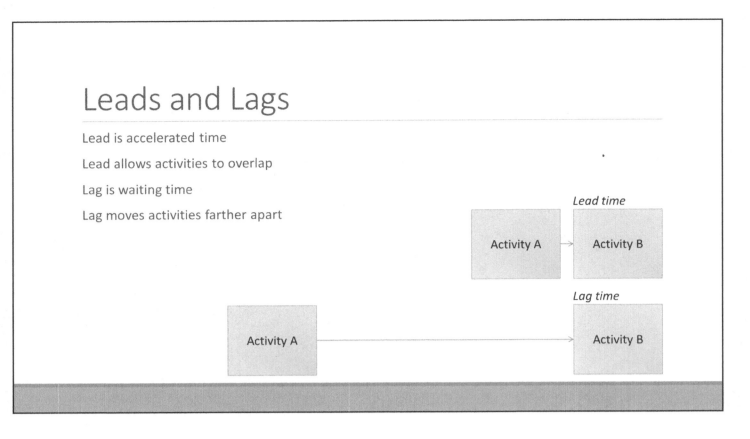

Sometimes there are activities that should have a delay between them. For example, you prime the walls and then you need to wait 24 hours for the primer to cure before you can begin painting the walls. This "waiting time" is called lag time. Lag time is considered positive time, because you are moving the successor tasks farther away from the predecessor task in the project.

The inverse of lag time is called lead time. Lead time is when you allow two activities to move closer together and even overlap. For example, let's say you were remodeling a huge hotel ballroom. You believe it'll take five days to prime all of the walls in this ballroom. You wouldn't necessarily need all of the walls primed before you could begin the activity of painting. We could sequence the activities as finish-to-start but add lead time to the painting activity to overlap the priming activity.

Network Templates

Previous projects

Pre-populated templates

Organizational process assets

Sequencing Outputs

Required work should be scheduled

Finish-to-start relationship most common

Activity sequence is not the schedule

PERT charts aren't PNDs

Updating the PND

Changes to the project scope

Updates to the scope baseline

Updates to the activities list

Updates to the PND

ESTIMATE THE ACTIVITY RESOURCES

ACTIVITIES WILL NEED PEOPLE, EQUIPMENT, TOOLS, FACILITIES AND
MATERIALS IN ORDER TO BE COMPLETE

Resources include materials, equipment, and people. After the project manager and the project team have worked together to determine the sequence of the activities, they now have to determine which resources are needed for each activity, as well as how much of each resource. As you can guess, resource estimating goes hand in hand with cost estimating. This lecture will define:

- Considering the project work
- Examining the labor availability
- Estimating the resource need
- Creating a resource calendar

6.4 Estimate Activity Resources

Resources to complete activities
- People
- Equipment
- Materials
- Facilities

ITTO: Estimate Activity Resources

Inputs	Tools & Techniques	Outputs
Schedule management plan	Expert judgment	Activity resource requirements
Activity list	Alternative analysis	Resource breakdown structure
Activity attributes	Published estimating data	Project documents updates
Resource calendars	Bottom-up estimating	
Risk register	Project management software	
Activity cost estimates		
Enterprise environmental factors		
Organizational process assets		

Resource Availability

Resource calendar

Negotiate for resources

Move the related activity

Delay the activity or project

Find alternative resources

Activity Resource Needs

Effort-driven activities

Fixed-duration activities

Effort can affect completion date

Law of Diminishing Returns

_____

_____

_____

_____

_____

_____

_____

Examining Project Calendars

Project calendar – when the project work takes places

Resource calendar – when resources are available

Creating a Resource Breakdown Structure

Like the WBS

Utilization of resources

Expose resource constraints

Identify resource needs

"To succeed in life, you need two things: ignorance and confidence."

– Mark Twain

ESTIMATE THE ACTIVITY DURATIONS

ESTIMATE HOW LONG EACH ACTIVITY WILL TAKE TO COMPLETE

First, you identify the activities, sequence the activities, define the resources, and then estimate durations. These processes are needed to complete the project schedule and the project duration estimate. These four processes are iterated as more information becomes available. If the proposed schedule is acceptable, the project can move forward. If the proposed schedule takes too long, the scheduler can use a few strategies to compress the project. We'll discuss the art of scheduling in a few moments.

Activity duration estimates, like the activity list and the WBS, don't come from the project manager—they come from the people completing the work. The estimates may also undergo progressive elaboration. In this section, we'll examine the approach to completing activity duration estimates, the basis of these estimates, and allow for activity list updates. In order to predict when the project will end you'll need to examine project activity duration. That's what this module covers:

- Estimating the project duration
- Using analogous estimates
- Using parametric estimates
- Using three-point estimates
- Creating a management reserve

6.5 Estimate Activity Durations

Level of detail leads to accuracy

Activity lists

Activity resource requirements

Activity attributes

Resource capabilities

Organizational process assets

ITTO: Estimate Activity Durations

Inputs	Tools & Techniques	Outputs
Schedule management plan	Expert judgment	Activity duration estimates
Activity list	Analogous estimating	Project documents updates
Activity attributes	Parametric estimating	
Activity resource requirements	Three-point estimating	
Resource calendars	Group decision-making techniques	
Project scope statement	Reserve analysis	
Risk register		
Resource breakdown structure		
Enterprise environmental factors		
Organizational process assets		

Analogous Estimating

Creates an analogy

Similar project work

Historical information

Top-down estimating

If your organization has completed similar projects there's no reason to start an estimate from scratch. An analogous cost estimate uses the historical information of past projects to predict the costs of the current project. This is sometimes called a top-down estimate.

_____

_____

_____

_____

_____

_____

_____

Parametric Estimating

Parameter for estimating

Repetitive work

Learning curve

If there's a cost parameter within the project the project manager should use it. Examples include cost per software license, cost per hour, cost per square foot of construction. A parametric model allows the project manager to multiply the units times the parameter to create a cost estimate.

_____

_____

_____

_____

_____

_____

_____

Three-Point Estimates

Finds an average of
- Optimistic
- Most likely
- Pessimistic
- Also called triangular distribution

(O+ML+P)/3=Estimate

(25+45+75)/3=48.33 hours

Some project managers use what's called a three-point estimate to predict how long the project duration will take. This estimate type uses three points for each work package: the optimistic estimated time, the most likely estimated time, and the pessimistic estimated time to predict how long each work package will take to complete. The project manager then finds and uses the average of the three points to estimate how long the project work will take to complete.

PERT Estimates

Program Evaluation and Review Technique

Also called beta distribution

(O+(4ML)+P)/6=estimate

(25+(4x45)+75)/6=46.66 hours

The Program Evaluation and Review Technique (PERT) is similar to the three-point estimate. PERT uses a weighted average while the three-point estimate does not. Here's the formula for PERT: (Optimistic + (4 x Most Likely) + Pessimistic)/6.

Activity: Task A has an Optimistic time of 28 hours, a Most Likely time of 45 hours, and a Pessimistic time of 80 hours. Find the predicted time for this task using PERT and using a three-point estimate.

_____

_____

_____

_____

_____

_____

_____

Reserve Time

Parkinson's Law

10-15 percent of project duration

Allotted to time overruns

Parkinson's Law states that work will expand to fill the amount of time it is allotted. Here's an example: you, the project manager, are working with your project team to determine how long each activity will take to complete. Suzie knows that an assignment she'll be completing for the project will probably take 32 hours to complete. Suzie, however, knows that there might be some problems, some snags, or some other delay, so she "pads" the duration estimate by eight hours and tells you it'll likely take her 40 hours to complete the assignment.

Guess what? It'll magically take 40 hours to complete the work. Suzie will either complete the work in 32 hours and not tell you she's done because she reported it'll take 40 hours or she'll ease through the work and use all 40 hours to complete the 32-hour assignment. Another possibility is that Suzie won't start on the actual work until hour eight and she'll pray and hope nothing goes awry in the assignment. The worst possible scenario is that she'll wait until hour eight to begin, things do go awry, and she'll require more than the allotted 40 hours for the work.

_____

_____

_____

_____

_____

_____

_____

DEVELOP THE PROJECT SCHEDULE

DEFINE WHEN THE PROJECT ACTIVITIES WILL TAKE PLACE – AND FIND FLOAT AND THE CRITICAL PATH

The project manager, the project team, and possibly even the key stakeholders, will examine the inputs previously described and apply the techniques discussed in this section to create a feasible schedule for the project. The point of the project schedule is to complete the project scope in the shortest possible time without incurring exceptional costs, risks, or a loss of quality.

Creating the project schedule is part of the planning process group. It is calendar-based and relies on both the project network diagram and the accuracy of time estimates. When the project manager creates the project schedule, she'll also reference the risk register. The identified risks and their associated responses can affect the sequence of the project work and when the project work can take place. In addition, if a risk comes to fruition, the risk event may affect the scheduling of the resources and the project completion date. Do you know how to calculate float? If not, this is the module you'll want to spend some time in. This module includes:

- Examining the project network
- Finding the critical path and float
- Worksheet: Float Exercise
- Compressing the project schedule
- Simulating the project work
- Leveling the project resources
- Using the critical chain methodology
- Applying calendars and updating the project schedule

_____

_____

_____

_____

6.6 Develop Schedule

Defines the sequence of events

Durations of the activities and project

Determines when resources are needed

Establishes logical relationships between activities

ITTO: Develop Schedule

Inputs	Tools & Techniques	Outputs
Schedule management plan	Schedule network analysis	Schedule baseline
Activity list	Critical path method	Project schedule
Activity attributes	Critical chain method	Schedule data
Project schedule network diagrams	Resource optimization techniques	Project calendars
Activity resource requirements	Modeling techniques	PM plan updates
Resource calendars	Leads and lags	Project documents updates
Activity duration estimates	Schedule compression	
Project scope statement	Scheduling tool	
Risk register		
Project staff assignments		
Resource breakdown structure		
Enterprise environmental factors		
Organizational process assets		

Project Constraints

Must start on

Must finish on

Start no earlier than

Start no later than

Finish no earlier than

Finish no later than

Assumptions and Scheduling

New work

Risks

Force majeure

Labor

Effort

Risks and the Schedule

Risk is an uncertain event or condition

Knowns and unknowns

Risk analysis affects completion

Risk affects costs and time

Determining the Project Timeline

- PERT charts
- Project calendars
- Effort and efficiency
- Alternative identifications

ID	Task Name	Duration
1	Establish the need	2d
2	Set target date	1d
3	Establish leadtimes	1d
4	Book venue	1d
5	Choose advert location	1d
6	Agree format	2d
7	Devise tests	5d
8	Job description	2d
9	Set criteria	1d
10	Write advert	2d
11	Place advert	1d
12	Shortlist	3d
13	Invite candidates	1d
14	Conduct interviews	3d
15	Take decision	1d
16		
17		

Project Network Diagram

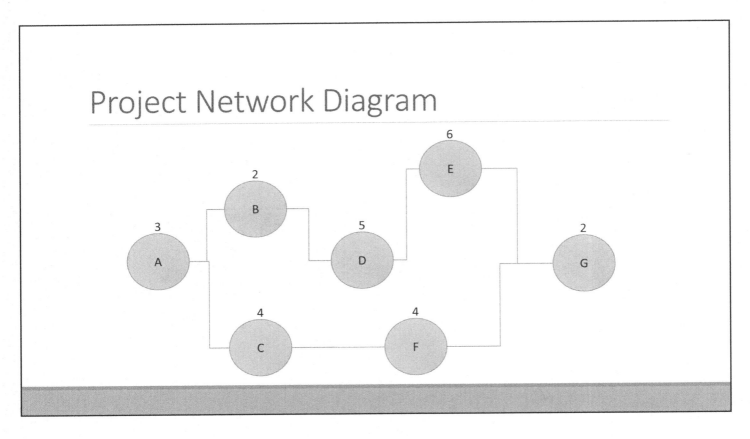

Once you have created the activity list you and the project team can work together to create a project network diagram. A project network diagram is a visual representation of the order of the activities needed in order to complete the project. Most project network diagrams use a technique called the precedence diagramming method – which is just a way to say that a project activity has predecessors and successors. A predecessor is an activity that must be completed before a successor activity can begin.

Schedule Network Analysis

Find earliest completion date

Find latest completion date

Find opportunities to shift resources

Find opportunities to delay

SWOT

Project Network Diagram

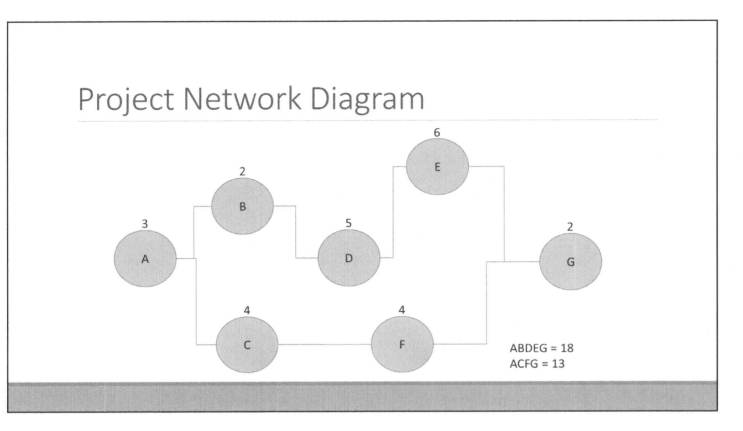

A benefit of using the project network diagram is that you can identify the critical path. The critical path is the a path in the network diagram that cannot be delayed or the project will be late. You can find the critical path by using project management software, such as Primavera or Microsoft Project. You can manually find the critical path, if you really want to, by identifying all of the paths in the project network diagram and then adding up the duration of all nodes used in that path.

Finding Float

Free float   An activity can be delayed without delaying the early start of any successor activities

Total float   An activity can be delayed without delaying project completion

Project float   A project can be delayed without passing the customer-expected completion date

The idea of allowing some of the activities to be delayed, or rather taking advantage of delaying non-critical path activities is called float — sometimes also called slack. Float is the opportunity to delay an activity.

_____

_____

_____

_____

_____

_____

_____

Forward Pass: ES+du-1=EF

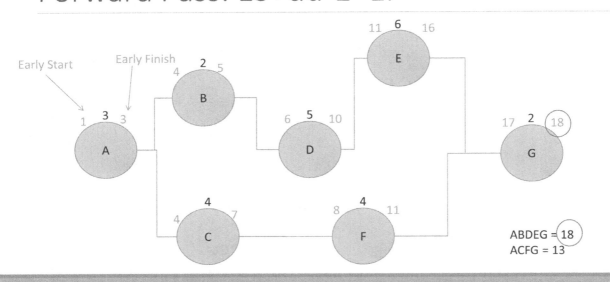

ABDEG = 18
ACFG = 13

Backward Pass: LF-du+1=LS

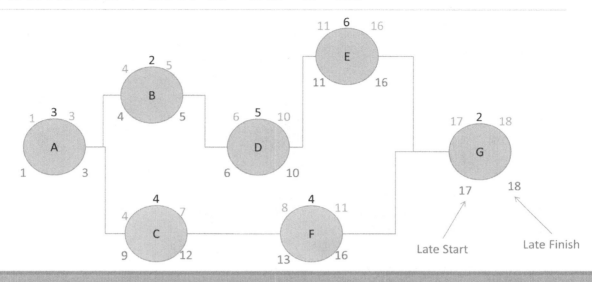

Late Start

Late Finish

Backward Pass: LF-du+1=LS

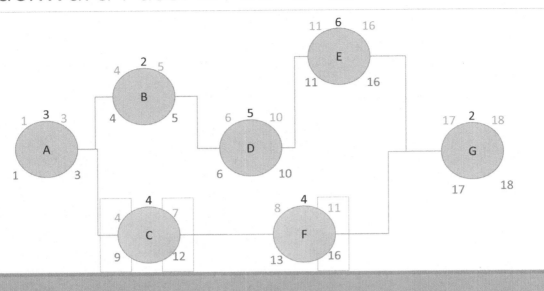

Practicing Float

Float Exercise worksheet

Create your own samples

Only a few questions on float

PRACTICE ACTIVITY

PRACTICE FINDING FLOAT AND THE CRITICAL PATH

Float, or slack, is the amount of time an activity can be delayed without postponing the project's completion. Technically, there are three different types of float:

- Free float: This is the total time a single activity can be delayed without affecting the early start of any successor activities
- Total float: This is the total time an activity can be delayed without affecting project completion.
- Project float: This is the total time the project can be delayed without passing the customer-expected completion date.

There are a couple of different approaches to calculating float. I'm sharing the approach that I learned and that I think is the best approach. You may have learned a different method that you prefer. You won't hurt my feelings if you use your method to get the same result as my method. What's most important is that you understand the concepts of forward and backward passes, and that you can find the critical path and float in a simple network diagram.

Most project management software will automatically calculate float. On the PMP exam, however, candidates will be expected to calculate float manually. Don't worry—it's not too tough.

Activity: Practice Float

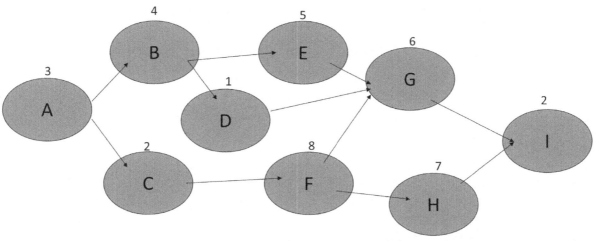

Float Questions

If activity E is delayed two days how much can activity G be delayed?

If the duration of activity D takes three additional days how long will the project take to finish?

If activity F takes 11 days to complete what is the earliest day that activity G will be able to finish?

Activity Answer: Practice Float

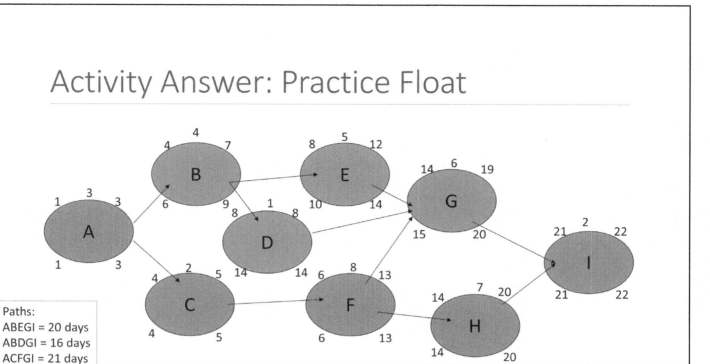

Paths:
ABEGI = 20 days
ABDGI = 16 days
ACFGI = 21 days
ACFHI = 22 days

Float Question Answers

If activity E is delayed two days how much can activity G be delayed?

- Zero! If Activity E is delayed two days then the path will equal 22 days in duration.

If the duration of activity D takes three additional days how long will the project take to finish?

- The project will still take 22 days total as there are six days of float available for Activity D.

If activity F takes 11 days to complete what is the earliest day that activity G will be able to finish?

- Activity G couldn't start until Day 17 and will last six days. The earliest Activity G could finish would be Day 22.

Using the Critical Chain Method

Focuses on project delivery date

Consider the availability of resources

Adds buffer on activities to account for unknowns and resources

Critical path doesn't consider if resources are available

Using the Critical Chain Method

Focuses on project delivery date

Consider the availability of resources

Adds buffer on activities to account for unknowns and resources

Critical path doesn't consider if resources are available

CONSIDER RESOURCE AVAILABILITY FOR SCHEDULING

RESOURCE AVAILABILITY AFFECTS PROJECT DURATION AND PROJECT SCHEDULE COMPRESSION

Schedule compression is also a mathematical approach to scheduling. The trick with schedule compression, as its name implies, is calculating ways the project can get done sooner than expected. Consider a construction project. The project may be slated to last eight months, but due to the cold and nasty weather typical of month seven, the project manager needs to rearrange activities, where possible, to end the project as soon as possible.

In some instances, the relationship between activities cannot be changed due to hard logic or external dependencies. The relationships are fixed and must remain as scheduled. Now consider the same construction company that is promised a bonus if they can complete the work by the end of month seven. Now there's incentive to complete the work, but there's also the fixed relationship between activities.

To apply duration compression, the performing organization can rely on two different methods. These methods can be used independently or together, and are applied to activities or to the entire project based on need, risk, and cost.

_____

_____

_____

_____

_____

_____

_____

_____

Using Resource Leveling Heuristics

Limits labor in time period

Often extends the project schedule

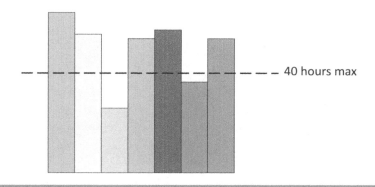

40 hours max

Schedule Compression

Crashing adds people and costs

Fast tracking adds risk and overlaps

Monte Carlo Simulation

Crashing means that the project manager will add labor to the project work in order to complete it faster than originally planned. Fast tracking allows entire phases of a project to overlap. You might see this in larger construction projects where the foundation of a building isn't completed all the way around but the skeleton of the building is being constructed just steps behind the foundation phase. The problem, and danger, with fast tracking is that it increases risk in the project. If there's a problem with the first phase deliverable it's likely to impact all of the phases that have overlapped it.

Develop Schedule Process

Milestone charts

Bar charts

Project schedule network diagrams

Visualize the project work

_____

_____

_____

_____

_____

_____

_____

_____

6.7 Control Schedule

Schedule Change Control System

Measuring project performance

Examining schedule variance

Updating the project schedule

Corrective actions

Lessons learned

Like most things in a project, the project manager will need to work to control the schedule from slipping off its baseline. A schedule control system is a formal approach to managing changes to the project schedule. It considers the conditions, reasons, requests, costs, and risks of making changes. It includes methods of tracking changes, approval levels based on thresholds, and the documentation of approved or declined changes. The schedule control system process is part of integrated change management. This lecture will help you to understand:

- Examining the project schedule characteristics
- Examining the schedule baseline
- Reporting the project progress
- Using a schedule change control system
- Examining schedule variances
- Using schedule comparison bar charts

_____

_____

_____

_____

_____

_____

_____

ITTO: Control Schedule

Inputs	Tools & Techniques	Outputs
Project management plan	Performance reviews	Work performance information
Project schedule	Project management software	Schedule forecasts
Work performance data	Resource optimization techniques	Change requests
Project calendars	Modeling techniques	Project management plan updates
Schedule data	Leads and lags	Project documents updates
Organizational process assets	Schedule compression	Organizational process assets updates
	Scheduling tool	

Measuring Project Performance

Value tied to percentage of work completed

Planned value – what the project should be worth

Estimate to complete

Estimate at completion

Milestones

Key deliverables

Performance Reviews

Trend analysis

Critical path analysis

Critical chain method

Earned value management

Schedule forecasting

"After every difficulty, ask yourself two questions: "What did I do right?" and "What would I do differently?"

— Brian Tracy

Learning Game!

http://www.instructing.com/wp-content/pub/6/story.html

Chapter exam

PLAN PROJECT COST MANAGEMENT

ESTIMATING, BUDGETING, AND CONTROLLING THE COSTS OF THE PROJECT

You need a plan just for project costs. You need a plan that will help you define what policies you and the project team have to adhere to in regard to costs, a plan that documents how you get to spend project money, and a plan for how cost management will happen throughout your entire project. Well, you're in luck! This plan, a subsidiary plan of the project management plan, is the project cost management plan. You'll need to understand all about the project's cost management plan for your PMP exam. This lecture covers:

- Creating the cost management plan
- Adhering to organizational policies and procedures
- Relying on organizational process assets and enterprise environmental factors

_____

_____

_____

_____

_____

_____

_____

_____

7.1 Plan Cost Management

Subsidiary plan of the project management plan

Addresses three cost management processes:
- How costs are estimates
- How the project budget is managed
- How costs will be controlled

ITTO: Plan Cost Management

Inputs	Tools & Techniques	Outputs
Project management plan	Expert judgment	Cost management plan
Project charter	Analytical techniques	
Enterprise environmental factors	Meetings	
Organizational process assets		

Cost Management Plan

Cost estimating approach

Budgeting approach

Cost control measures

Level of precision

Units of measure

Organizational procedure links

Control thresholds

Rules of performance measurement

Reporting formats

Process descriptions

Like the schedule management plan, the cost management plan defines the process for controlling and managing costs (instead of time). The cost management plan does acknowledge the expenses within the project and how variances to those expenses will be managed and communicated.

ESTIMATE PROJECT COSTS

PROJECT COSTS MUST BE ESTIMATED BASED ON THE INFORMATION AVAILABLE.

Assuming that the project manager and the project team are working together to create the cost estimates, there are many inputs to the cost-estimating process. For your PMI exam, it would behoove you to be familiar with these inputs because these are often the supporting details for the cost estimate the project management team creates. Cost estimating uses several tools and techniques. You'll learn in this module:

- Following the organizational process assets
- Building a cost management plan
- Creating an analogous estimate
- Determining resource cost rates
- Create a bottom-up estimate
- Building a parametric estimate
- Using the PMIS
- Analyzing vendor bids
- Considering the contingency reserve
- Presenting the cost estimate

Estimating the Project Costs

Predictions based on current information

Cost tradeoffs and risks considered
- Cost versus buy
- Cost versus lease
- Sharing resources

Level of accuracy
- Rough order of magnitude estimate
- Budget estimate
- Definitive estimate

All categories of costs estimated

Everyone wants to know how much your project will cost. The more information you have available, such as the project scope statement or the WBS, the more reliable your cost estimates will be.

ITTO: Estimate Costs

Inputs	Tools & Techniques	Outputs
Cost management plan	Expert judgment	Activity cost estimates
HR management plan	Analogous estimating	Basis of estimates
Scope baseline	Parametric estimating	Project documents updates
Project schedule	Bottom-up estimating	
Risk register	Three-point estimating	
Enterprise environmental factors	Reserve analysis	
Organizational process assets	Cost of quality	
	Project management software	
	Vendor bid analysis	
	Group decision-making techniques	

Creating a Cost Estimate

Rough order of magnitude
- -25% to +75%

Budget estimate
- -10% to +25%

Definitive estimate
- -5% to +10%

As a general rule, project cost estimates move through three cost estimates:

1. Rough order of magnitude – This is the ballpark estimate. These are the wild estimates where the project sponsor pitches an idea and asks for a ballpark price. A rough order of magnitude (ROM) estimate can vary -25 percent up to +75 percent of the fee. As expected, ROM estimates are not very reliable.
2. Budget estimate – As the project moves into the initial planning and more specifics are known about the project a budget estimate can be created. Budget estimates may range from -10 percent to +75 percent.
3. Definitive estimates – Finally an estimate we can depend on. The definitive estimate is the most accurate of all three progressions of project cost estimates. Its range of variance can be from -5 percent to +10 percent. What makes this estimate type so reliable? The work breakdown structure has to be in existence in order to create a definitive estimate. So while the definitive estimate is the most accurate it also takes the longest to complete. (If you're thinking this sounds an awful lot like the bottom-up estimate you're right – it's the same darn thing.)

Four Cost Categories

Direct costs

Indirect costs

Variable costs

Fixed costs

Project Schedule and Cost Estimating

Resource availability

Timing of procurement of resources

Cost of project financing

Time-sensitive costs

Seasonal cost variations

Analogous Estimating

Top down approach

Quick, but unreliable

Historical information

Project A

Project B

If your organization has completed similar projects there's no reason to start an estimate from scratch. An analogous cost estimate uses the historical information of past projects to predict the costs of the current project. This is sometimes called a top-down estimate.

_____

_____

_____

_____

_____

_____

_____

_____

Parametric Estimating

Based on a cost parameter

$329 per software license

$4500 per metric ton

Consider the learning curve

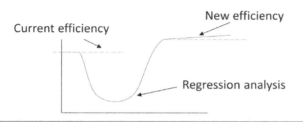

Current efficiency

New efficiency

Regression analysis

If there's a cost parameter within the project the project manager should use it. Examples include cost per software license, cost per hour, cost per square foot of construction. A parametric model allows the project manager to multiply the units times the parameter to create a cost estimate.

Bottom-Up Estimating

Based on WBS creation

Also called a definitive estimate

Cost of each work package

Cost of work packages are rolled-up

A bottom-up estimate starts at zero and accounts for each deliverable in the project's WBS. This is the most accurate estimate type, but it takes the longest amount of time to complete.

Three-Point Cost Estimates

Average of cost

(Optimistic + Most Likely + Pessimistic)/3

PERT
- (O+(4M)+P)/6

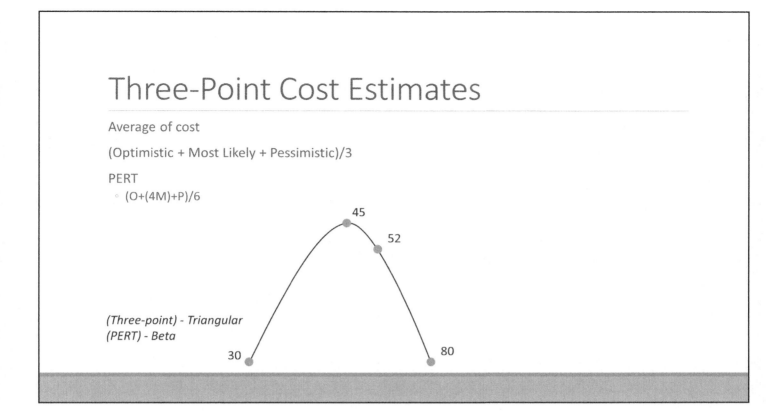

(Three-point) - Triangular
(PERT) - Beta

Activity: Consider a project that has a task with an optimistic estimate of 25 hours, a most likely estimate of 55 hours, and a pessimistic estimate of 80 hours.

- Using PERT, what's the predicted duration of the task?
- Using a three-point estimate, what's the predicted duration of the task?
- What's the difference between the two estimates?

_____

_____

_____

_____

_____

_____

_____

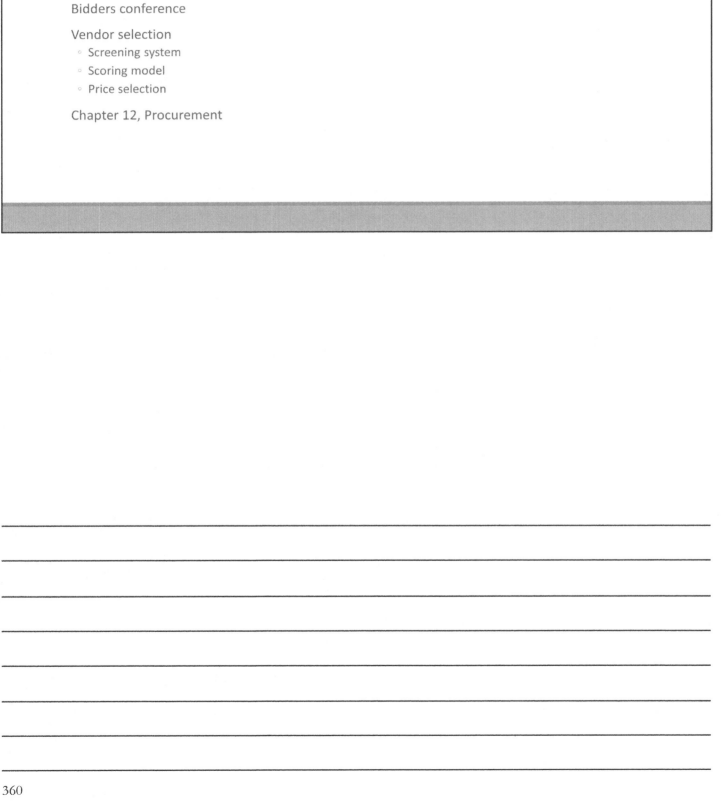

Vendor Bid Analysis

Should cost estimates (Third party estimates)

Statement of Work (SOW)

Bidders conference

Vendor selection
- Screening system
- Scoring model
- Price selection

Chapter 12, Procurement

Cost Estimate Results

Activity cost estimates

Basis of estimates

- Supporting detail
- Assumptions and constraints
- Range of variance
- Confidence level of estimate

CREATE THE PROJECT BUDGET

THE PROJECT BUDGET IS THE ACTUAL AMOUNT OF
FUNDS AVAILABLE FOR THE PROJECT EXPENSES

Now that the project estimate has been created, it's time to create the official cost budget. Cost budgeting is really cost aggregation, which means the project manager will be assigning specific dollar amounts for each of the scheduled activities or, more likely, for each of the work packages in the WBS. The aggregation of the work package cost equates to the summary budget for the entire project. There is a difference between what was estimated and what's actually being spent on the project. This lecture defines:

- Aggregating the project costs
- Completing project cost reconciliation
- Creating the project cost baseline
- Examining the project cash flow

7.3 Determine Budget

Aggregating the estimated costs

Cost of work packages and activities

Authorized cost baseline

Excludes management reserves

Performance measured against budget

ITTO: Determine Budget

Inputs	Tools & Techniques	Outputs
Cost management plan	Cost aggregation	Cost baseline
Scope baseline	Reserve analysis	Project funding requirements
Activity cost estimates	Expert judgment	Project documents updates
Basis of estimates	Historical relationships	
Project schedule	Funding limit reconciliation	
Resource calendars		
Risk register		
Agreements		
Organizational process assets		

Let's reflect on that summary budget for a moment. Here in this big overview of project management it's easy for me to say blah – you need a summary budget based on X, Y, and Z. I'm not a simpleton; I know that organizations often slap a price tag on a project based on historical information, shallow research, or based on what's left in the bank account to get a project done. Every organization works differently regarding how projects get funded. The note here is to learn how your project gets funded and then act accordingly.

Reserve Analysis

Contingency reserve

Management reserve

Unknown unknowns

Not part of the cost baseline, but part of the project budget

Reserve Analysis

Contingency reserve

Management reserve

Unknown unknowns

Not part of the cost baseline, but part of the project budget

Creating the Project Budget

Actual cost of the project

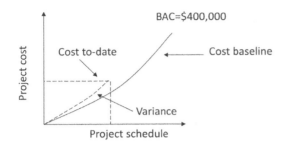

Relying on Historical Relationships

Both parametric and analogous are historical-based estimates

The historical information affects the estimates
- Accuracy of historical information
- Quantifiable parameters
- Models are scalable for any size project

Funding Limit Reconciliation

Reconcile planned and actual costs

Cost variances

Corrective actions

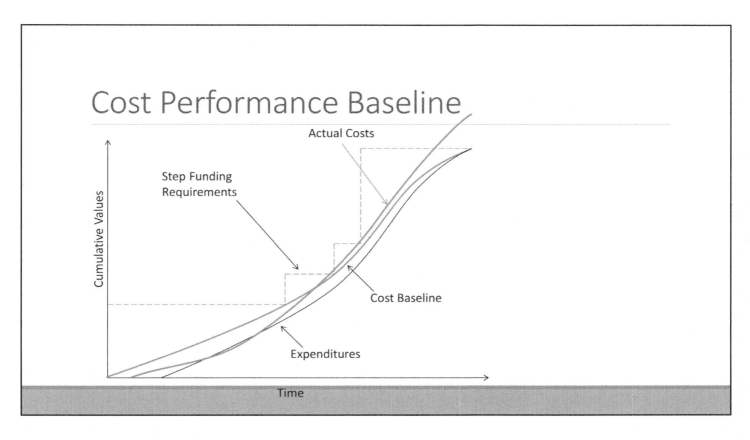

Scope verification works along with the concept of step funding. When a phase is complete and scope verification approves the phase a new round of funding is provided to the project. The above figure demonstrates the curve of the project schedule and costs while the "stair steps" represent the monies to pay for the materials and labor to reach each phase of the project.

Project Funding Requirements

Total funding requirements

Periodic funding requirements

Anticipated liabilities

Management reserves

7.4 Control Costs

Monitoring status of the project

Managing changes to the cost baseline

Variance management and corrective actions

Balancing project risk and reward

_____

_____

_____

_____

_____

_____

_____

_____

CONTROL PROJECT COST

COST MUST BE CONTROLLED WITHIN THE PROJECT AND CONSIDER CHANGES, ERRORS AND OMISSIONS, AND SHOW PROJECT PERFORMANCE

Once a project has been funded, it's up to the project manager and the project team to work effectively and efficiently to control costs. This means doing the work right the first time. It also means, and this is tricky, avoiding scope creep and undocumented changes, as well as getting rid of any non-value-added activities. Basically, if the project team is adding components or features that aren't called for in the project, they're wasting time and money.

Cost control focuses on controlling the ability of costs to change and on how the project management team may allow or prevent cost changes from happening. When a change does occur, the project manager must document the change and the reason why it occurred and, if necessary, create a variance report. Cost control is concerned with understanding why the cost variances, both good and bad, have occurred. The "why" behind the variances allows the project manager to make appropriate decisions on future project actions. Managing cost control is an ongoing activity within a project. This lecture defines cost control, including earned value management. You'll learn:

- Working with a cost change control system
- Measuring project performance
- Earned Value Management fundamentals
- Finding project variances
- Calculating the project performance
- Forecasting the project performance
- Earned Value Management formula review

Cost Control

Influence change factors

Change requests

Managing changes (approved/unapproved)

Tracking costs

Isolate variances for study

Earned value management

Communicating cost status

Cost overruns and allowed variances

ITTO: Control Costs

Inputs	Tools & Techniques	Outputs
Project management plan	Earned value management	Work performance information
Project funding requirements	Forecasting	Cost forecasts
Work performance data	To-complete performance index (TCPI)	Change requests
Organizational process assets	Performance reviews	Project management plan updates
	Project management software	Project documents updates
	Reserve analysis	Organizational process assets updates

Measuring Project Performance

Earned Value Management

Forecast

Measure performance

Suite of formulas

A few PMP questions

EVM Foundation

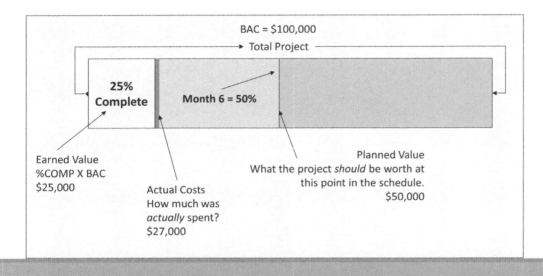

BAC = $100,000

Total Project

25% Complete

Month 6 = 50%

Earned Value
%COMP X BAC
$25,000

Actual Costs
How much was
actually spent?
$27,000

Planned Value
What the project *should* be worth at
this point in the schedule.
$50,000

Finding the Variances

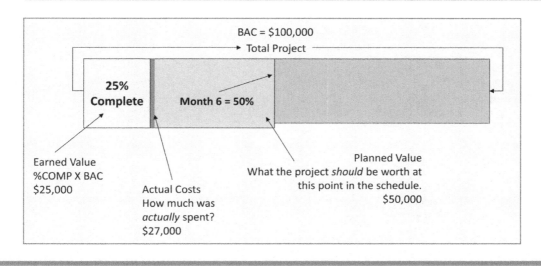

Activity: You are the project manager for your company. Your project has a budget of $450,600 and you are twenty percent complete today. You were, however, supposed to be 25 percent complete. In addition, you've spent $99,000 to reach this point in the project.

Based on this information find these values:

- Earned value
- Planned value
- Cost variance
- Schedule variance

_____

_____

_____

_____

_____

_____

_____

_____

Measuring Performance

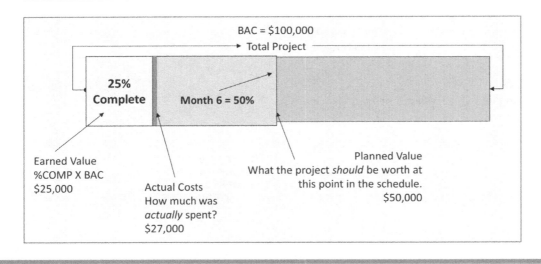

BAC = $100,000
Total Project

25% Complete

Month 6 = 50%

Earned Value
%COMP X BAC
$25,000

Actual Costs
How much was
actually spent?
$27,000

Planned Value
What the project *should* be worth at
this point in the schedule.
$50,000

Activity: You are the project manager for your company. Your project has a budget of $450,600 and you are twenty percent complete today. You were, however, supposed to be 25 percent complete. In addition, you've spent $99,000 to reach this point in the project.

Based on this information find these values:

- CPI
- SPI

_____

_____

_____

_____

_____

_____

_____

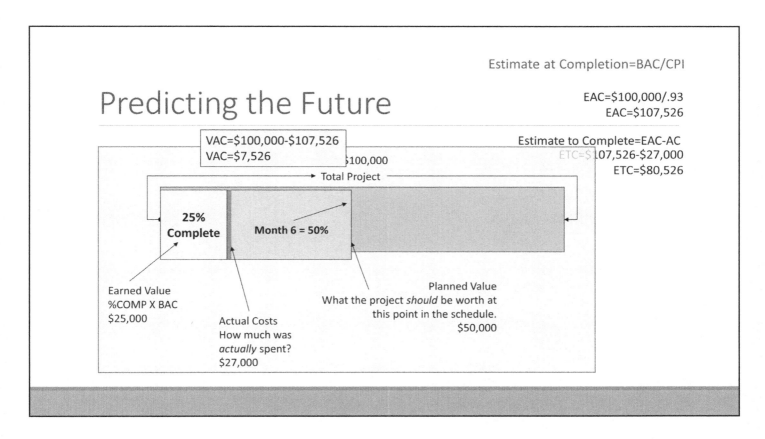

Predicting the Future

Activity: You are the project manager for your company. Your project has a budget of $450,600 and you are twenty percent complete today. You were, however, supposed to be 25 percent complete. In addition, you've spent $99,000 to reach this point in the project.

Based on this information find these values:

- Estimate at Completion
- Estimate to Complete
- Variance at Completion

_____

_____

_____

_____

_____

_____

_____

To-Complete Performance Index

Can you meet the BAC?

Can you meet the EAC?

TCPI=(BAC-EV)/(BAC-AC)

TCPI=(BAC-EV)/(EAC-AC)

TCPI=(BAC-EV)/(BAC-AC)

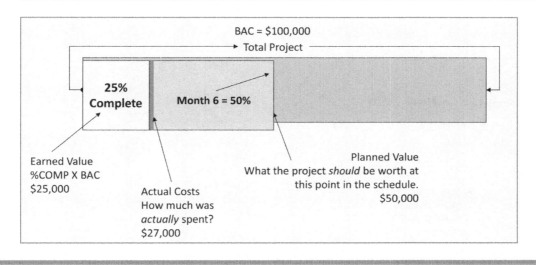

BAC = $100,000
Total Project

25% Complete

Month 6 = 50%

Earned Value
%COMP X BAC
$25,000

Actual Costs
How much was *actually* spent?
$27,000

Planned Value
What the project *should* be worth at this point in the schedule.
$50,000

TCPI=(BAC-EV)/(EAC-AC)

TCPI=($100,000-$25,000)/($107,526-$27,000)
TCPI=75,000/80,526
TCPI=.93

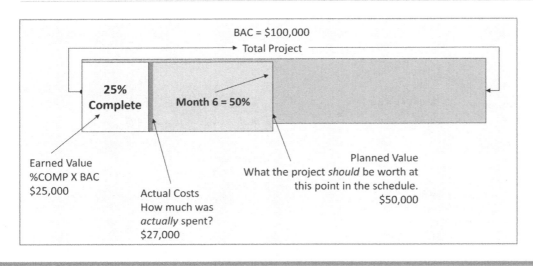

BAC = $100,000
Total Project

25% Complete

Month 6 = 50%

Earned Value
%COMP X BAC
$25,000

Actual Costs
How much was
actually spent?
$27,000

Planned Value
What the project *should* be worth at
this point in the schedule.
$50,000

Activity: You are the project manager for your company. Your project has a budget of $450,600 and you are twenty percent complete today. You were, however, supposed to be 25 percent complete. In addition, you've spent $99,000 to reach this point in the project.

Based on this information find these values:

*   To-Complete Performance Index using the BAC
*   To-Complete Performance Index using the EAC

Five EVM Rules

EV is first

Variance means subtract

Index means division

Less than one is bad in an index

Negative is bad in a variance

PRACTICE ACTIVITY

PRACTICE THE EARNED VALUE MANAGEMENT FORMULAS

Calculate for Earned Value Management

Consider that you are the project manager of the BGQ Project. This project has a budget of $1,560,000 and you are 30 percent complete. You are, however, supposed to be 35 percent complete today. In addition you've spent $512,000 to reach this point. Based on this information, solve for the following:

Earned value

Planned value

Cost variance

Schedule variance

Cost performance index

Schedule performance index

Estimate at completion

Estimate to complete

To-complete performance index (BAC)

To-complete performance index (EAC)

Variance at completion

_____

_____

_____

_____

_____

_____

_____

_____

Earned Value Management Answer

Consider that you are the project manager of the BGQ Project. This project has a budget of $1,560,000 and you are 30 percent complete. You are, however, supposed to be 35 percent complete today. In addition you've spent $512,000 to reach this point. Based on this information, solve for the following:

Earned value	468,000	Estimate at completion	1,706,667
Planned value	546,000	Estimate to complete	1,194,667
Cost variance	-44,000	To-complete performance index (BAC)	1.04
Schedule variance	-78,000	To-complete performance index (EAC)	0.91
Cost performance index	0.91	Variance at completion	-146,667
Schedule performance index	0.86		

Learning Game!

http://www.instructing.com/wp-content/pub/7/story.html

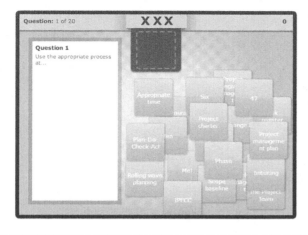

Chapter exam

PLAN PROJECT QUALITY MANAGEMENT

PLANNING TO ACHIEVE QUALITY, PERFORMING QUALITY
ASSURANCE AND QUALITY CONTROL WITHIN THE PROJECT

Quality planning is the process of first determining which quality standards are relevant to your project and then finding the best methods of adhering to those quality standards. This is a great example of project integration management, which was referred to earlier. Quality planning is core to the planning process group because each knowledge area has relevant standards that affect quality, and quality planning is integrated into each planning process. Quality can be an esoteric topic, but this lecture will help. You'll learn:

- Defining project quality
- Completing a cost-benefits analysis
- Benchmarking the project
- Performing a design of experiments
- Determining the cost of quality
- Creating the Quality Management Plan
- Establishing quality metrics
- Using quality checklists
- Creating a Process Improvement Plan
- Establishing a quality baseline

8.1 Plan Quality Management

Defines quality policy for the project

Defines quality assurance requirements

Defines how quality control activities will occur

Quality is the ability of product or service to satisfy stated and implied need and expectations. It's all about a fitness for use and conformance to requirements. The quality management plan defines what the project's expectations are, how quality assurance will be enforced, and how quality control will be administered within the project. Quality assurance is an organization-wide program, such as ISO 9000, that serves to prevent mistakes from entering the project. Quality control is an inspection-driven process that server to prevent mistakes from reaching the customer.

ITTO: Plan Quality Management

Inputs	Tools & Techniques	Outputs
Project management plan	Cost-benefit analysis	Quality management plan
Stakeholder register	Cost of quality	Process improvement plan
Risk register	Seven basic quality tools	Quality metrics
Requirements documentation	Benchmarking	Quality checklists
Enterprise environmental factors	Design of experiments	Project documents updates
Organizational process assets	Statistical sampling	
	Additional quality planning tools	
	Meetings	

Quality Management Approach

Top-down quality

Beware of:
- Overworking the project team
- Speeding through quality inspections

> "Follow effective actions with quiet reflection. From the quiet reflection will come even more effective action."
>
> — Peter Drucker

Quality v. Grade

Quality is about fulfilling requirements
- Project scope
- Product scope
- Implied needs

Grade is a category or rank
- Class of services
- Types of materials

A common misunderstanding when it comes to quality: quality and grade are not the same thing. Quality is about a fitness for use and conformance to project requirements. Grade is a ranking or measurement of a product or service. A perfect example is my flight. When I'm taking a long flight I typically opt for first class. If the flight is less than three hours, I'm in coach. Grade is the difference between first and coach. With each level of grade there are different expectations. I can have a quality flight in coach or first class – one isn't of more quality than the other, it's just their grade and purpose. Grade is centered on expectations while quality is centered on stated and implied needs.

Quality and Grade

Low quality is always a problem, low grade may not be.

Accuracy and Precision and Quality

Precision is a measure of exactness.

Accuracy is an assessment of correctness.

Precise measurements aren't necessarily accurate measurements.

Accurate measurements aren't necessarily precise measurements.

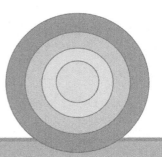

Imagine shooting five arrows at a bulls-eye target. Your five arrows all hit the center of bulls-eye - that's both precise and accurate. Meet Bob. Bob shoots his five arrows at his target. All of Bob's arrows hit in the upper right edge of the bulls-eye target in the outer ring. His shots were precise, as they were bunched together, but not accurate for the goal of the center of the target.

Jane shoots her five arrows. Hers all hit within the three rings closest to the bulls-eye, but not all in the center of the target. Her shots are accurate, but still not precise.

Now I shoot my five arrows and they're all over the place - except for the center of the target. My shots aren't accurate or precise.

Accuracy is hitting what's required. Precision is about repeatedly hitting the same performance. Both are about exactness, but it's more about hitting the correct goal and be able to repeat the hit.

_____

_____

_____

_____

_____

_____

_____

_____

Quality Project Management

Customer satisfaction
- Conformance to requirements
- Fitness for use

Prevention
- "Quality is planned into a project, not inspected in."

Management responsibility

Deming's "Plan-Do-Check-Act"

Quality Project Management

Kaizen technologies
- Continuous small improvements to reduce costs and ensure consistency

Marginal analysis
- Study of the cost of improvements to a product or service and how the costs contribute to an increase in revenue
- Marginal costs to create one more unit

Determining the Quality Policy

Formal quality approaches
- ISO programs
- Six Sigma
- Total Quality Management

If a quality policy doesn't exists the project manager must create one for the project.

Standards and Regulations

Standards are optional

Regulations are requirements

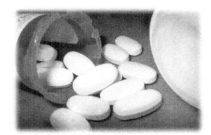 

Cost of Quality

Cost of conformance to requirements
- Safety measures
- Team development and training
- Proper materials and processes

Cost of non-conformance to requirements
- Liabilities, loss of life or limb
- Rework/scrap
- Lost business

USING SEVEN BASIC QUALITY TOOLS

THESE SEVEN TOOLS ARE USED FOR PROJECT QUALITY PLANNING, QUALITY ASSURANCE, AND QUALITY CONTROL

/

_____

_____

_____

_____

_____

_____

_____

Seven Basic Quality Tools

Cause and effect diagrams

Flowcharts

Check sheets

Pareto Diagrams

Histograms

Control charts

Scatter diagrams

Cause and Effect Diagrams

Ishikawa or fishbone

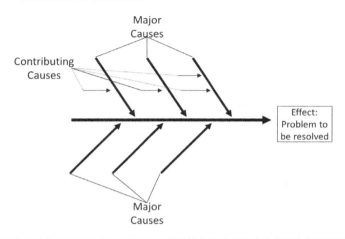

Flowcharting

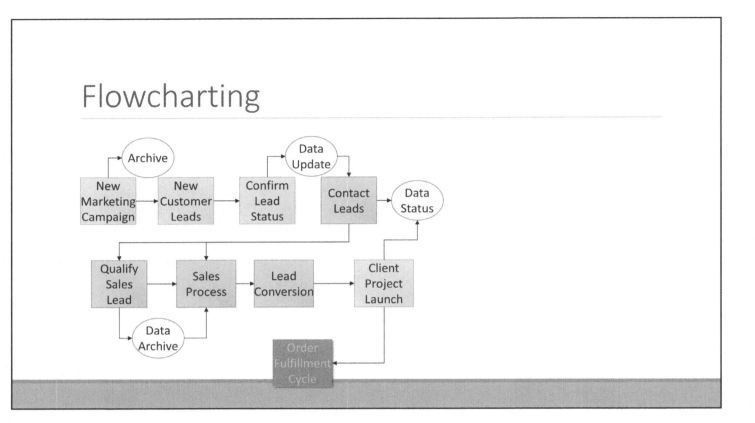

Pareto Chart

Histograms

Vertical bar chart show frequency

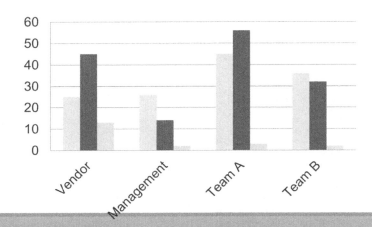

Control Charts

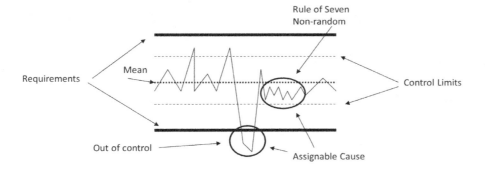

Control limits are usually ±3Σ

Creating a Scatter Diagram

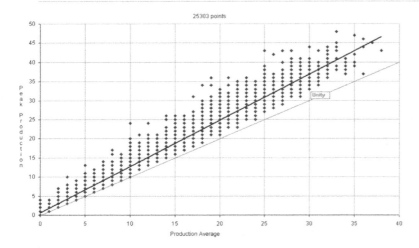

COMPLETE QUALITY MANAGEMENT PLANNING

PLANNING FOR QUALITY CREATES THE QUALITY
MANAGEMENT PLAN AND THE PROCESS IMPROVEMENT PLAN

_____

_____

_____

_____

_____

_____

_____

_____

Benchmarking the Project

Comparing two systems

Technology

Materials

Projects

Design of Experiments

Examines variables to determine the best outcome

One million postcards

The best results win

_____

_____

_____

_____

_____

_____

_____

Quality Planning Tools

Brainstorming – generate ideas

Affinity diagrams – logical grouping of ideas

Force field analysis – forces for and against

Nominal group technique – small groups of brainstorming then ideas reviewed by a larger group

Quality Management Plan

Quality assurance

Quality control

Continuous process improvement

Operational definitions
- Terminology
- Metrics
- Lexicon/glossary

Process Improvement Plan

Process boundaries

Process configuration

Process metrics

Targets for improvement

This subsidiary plan works to remove non-value added activities and components of the project's processes. Its goal is to improve and streamline the project's processes to help the project manager and the project team to better manage, control, and complete the project.

PERFORM QUALITY ASSURANCE

QUALITY ASSURANCE IS DOING THE
WORK CORRECTLY THE FIRST TIME – WITH QUALITY

Quality assurance (QA) is the sum of the creation and implementation of the plans by the project manager, the project team, and management to ensure that the project meets the demands of quality. QA is not something that is done only at the end of the project, but is done before and during the project as well. Quality management is prevention-driven; you want to do the work correctly the first time. Quality assurance is a prevention-driven activity. This lecture will explore that concept through these topics:

- Defining QA
- Performing a quality audit
- Examining the project processes
- Recommending corrective actions

_____

_____

_____

_____

_____

_____

_____

_____

8.2 Perform Quality Assurance

Auditing the quality requirements

Auditing results of quality control

Facilitates improvement of quality processes

QA is prevention driven

Being certain about quality in the product

The concept of quality assurance (QA) enters the project management stage. QA is a management-driven process to ensure that the project work is done right the first time. QA is a prevention-driven process. What's it preventing? It prevents mistakes, rework, corrective actions, and a breakdown of quality within the project deliverables. Quality assurance is comprised of four key points:

- Customer satisfaction
- Prevention
- Management provisions
- Plan-Do-Check-Act

_____

_____

_____

_____

_____

_____

_____

ITTO: Perform Quality Assurance

Inputs	Tools & Techniques	Outputs
Quality management plan	Quality management and control tools	Change requests
Process improvement plan	Quality audits	Project management plan updates
Quality metrics	Process analysis	Project documents updates
Quality control measurements		Organizational process assets updates
Project documents		

Quality Management and Control Tools

Affinity diagrams

Process decision program charts

Interrelationship diagraphs

Tree diagrams

Prioritization matrices

Activity network diagrams

Matrix diagrams

Completing a Quality Audit

Determine if project complies with organizational policies

- Best practices implemented?
- What nonconforming policies? What shortcomings?
- Share good practices with others?
- Offer assistance to improve processes?
- Highlight contributions?
- Lessons learned?

IMPLEMENT PROJECT QUALITY CONTROL

QUALITY CONTROL IS AN INSPECTION-DRIVEN ACTIVITY TO ENSURE THAT QUALITY EXISTS WITHIN THE PROJECT DELIVERABLES. ITS GOAL IS TO KEEP MISTAKES OUT OF THE HANDS OF THE CUSTOMER

This is the section of the project where the project manager and the project team have control and influence. Quality assurance (QA), for the most part, is specific to your organization, and the project manager doesn't have much control over the QA processes—he just has to do them. Quality control (QC), on the other hand, is specific to the project manager, so the project manager has lots of activities. Quality control is an inspection-driven activity and you'll learn that concept through this lecture.

- Performing quality control measurements
- Creating a cause and effect diagram
- Creating a control chart
- Completing project flowcharting
- Creating a histogram
- Examining a Pareto chart
- Creating a run chart
- Examining a scatter diagram
- Completing a statistical sampling
- Inspecting the project work
- Review defect repair
- Quality control and lessons learned

_____

_____

_____

_____

_____

8.3 Control Quality

Inspection-driven activity

Keep mistakes out of the customers' hands

Causal identification of poor quality

Validate quality for customer acceptance

Quality control is an inspection-driven process that the project manager and the project team do to keep mistakes out of the customer's hands. Its goal is to confirm that quality exists within the project deliverables and then to pass the deliverables on to the customers for their scope verification process. Should quality not exist within the project, then there's an analysis of why quality is missing and how quality can be injected back into the project.

_____

_____

_____

_____

_____

_____

_____

ITTO: Control Quality

Inputs	Tools & Techniques	Outputs
Project management plan	Seven basic quality tools	Quality control measurements
Quality metrics	Statistical sampling	Validated changes
Quality checklists	Inspection	Validated deliverables
Work performance data	Approved change requests review	Work performance information
Approved change requests		Change requests
Deliverables		Project management plan updates
Project documents		Project documents updates
Organizational process assets		Organizational process assets updates

How to do Quality Control:

Inspect the project deliverables

Measure the work

Utilize the seven basic quality tools

Try statistical sampling

_____

_____

_____

_____

_____

_____

_____

_____

Learning Game!

http://www.instructing.com/wp-content/pub/3/story.html

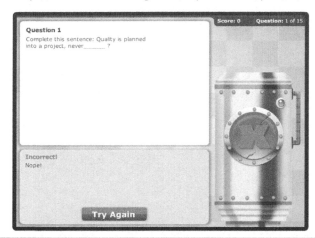

Chapter exam

PLAN PROJECT HUMAN RESOURCE MANAGEMENT

HOW TO MANAGE AND LEAD THE PEOPLE INVOLVED WITH THE PROJECT

The HR management plan defines what roles and responsibilities are needed on the project team and how those resources will be managed. This plan also defines how project team members will be brought onto and released from the project team.

_____

_____

_____

_____

_____

_____

_____

9.1 Plan Human Resource Management

Identifying project team needs

Reporting relationships

Assigning roles and responsibilities

Staffing management plan
- Staff acquisition
- Release of staff
- Consideration of organizational policies and structure

Have you noticed that every knowledge area for your PMI examination starts with a planning process? Hmmm, I hope so. Planning is an iterative process that begins early in the project and continues through the project management life cycle. Planning for project human resources is vital to a successful project. After all, you've got to plan how the project work will be completed and which resources will complete that work.

When it comes to planning human resources, the project manager is aiming to plan for several facets of the project. This lecture defines the planning for HR management:

- Defining human resource planning
- Examining the project interfaces
- Considering the project constraints
- Charting the organizational structure
- Defining the project roles and responsibilities
- Creating the Staffing Management Plan

ITTO: Plan Human Resource Management

Inputs	Tools & Techniques	Outputs
Project management plan	Organization charts and position descriptions	Human resource management plan
Activity resource requirements	Networking	
Enterprise environmental factors	Organizational theory	
Organizational process assets	Expert judgment	
	Meetings	

Organization Charts

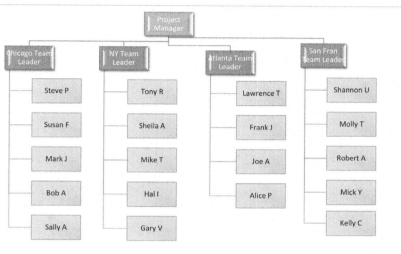

Matrix Chart

Activity	Team Member					
	Sam	Shelly	Ben	Frank	Lloyd	Mark
Web content	R	A		C	I	
Web design	A	R				
App development	I		A		R	
Security	I		R	I	I	A
Proofing				A		
Testing				R		
Payment system	I		I	I	I	R

Maslow's Hierarchy of Needs

A pyramid diagram showing Maslow's Hierarchy of Needs with the following levels from top to bottom:
- Self-actualization
- Esteem
- Social
- Safety
- Physiological

"*If the only tool you have is a hammer, you tend to see every problem as a nail.*"

– Abraham Maslow

Herzberg's Theory of Motivation

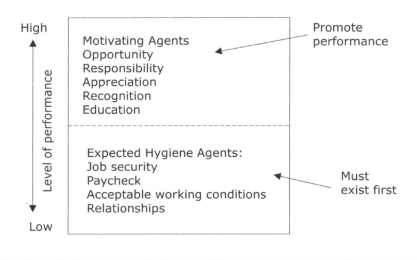

McGregor's X and Y

X People

Micromanagement
No trust
Lazy
Avoid work

Y People

Self-led
Motivated
Capable

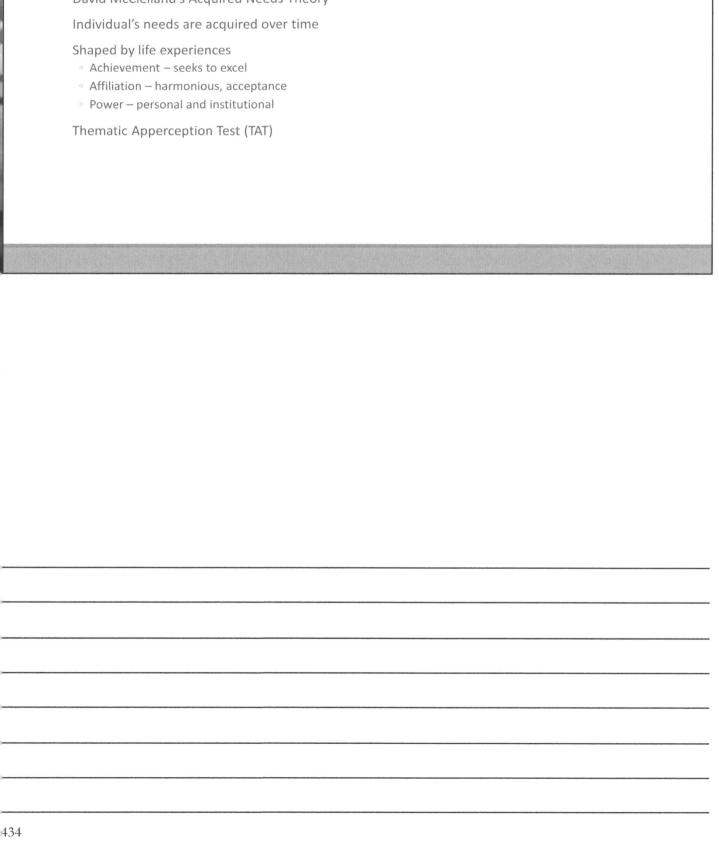

McClelland's Theory of Needs

David McClelland's Acquired Needs Theory

Individual's needs are acquired over time

Shaped by life experiences
- Achievement – seeks to excel
- Affiliation – harmonious, acceptance
- Power – personal and institutional

Thematic Apperception Test (TAT)

Other Theories

Ouchi's Theory Z
- Japanese Management Style
- Lifelong employment

Expectancy Theory
- People behave based on what they believe their behavior will bring them

Halo effect
- False belief based on a person's experiences

DEFINE ROLES AND RESPONSIBILITIES

WHO DOES WHAT AND WHO DECIDES WHAT

_____

_____

_____

_____

_____

_____

_____

Organizational Planning

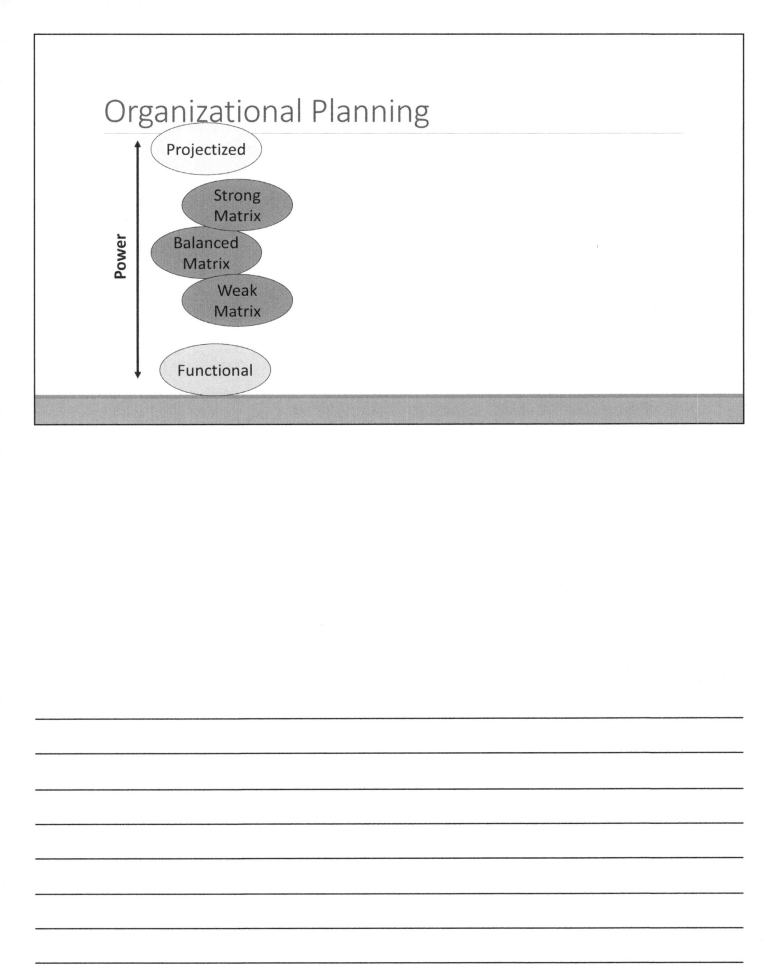

Roles and Responsibilities

Role – the label describing the portion of the project the person is accountable.

Authority – apply resources, make decisions, sign approvals.

Responsibility – the work that a project team member is expected to perform.

Competency – the skill and capacity required to complete project activities

Examining the Staffing Management Plan

Part of the human resource management plan

Staff acquisition

Resource calendars

Resource histogram

Staff release plan

Training needs

Recognition and rewards

Compliance and safety

ACQUIRE THE PROJECT TEAM

You need people to complete your project. But have you ever managed a project where the resources you wanted on the project were not available? Or have you managed a project where the resources you were assigned weren't the best resources to complete the project work? Staff acquisition is the process of getting the needed resources on the project team to complete the project work. It focuses on working within the policies and procedures of the performing organization to obtain the needed resources to complete the project work. Negotiation, communication, and political savvy are the keys to getting the desired resources on the project team. For your PMP exam, it's important to understand that how a project manager acquires the project team can vary by organization. You'll need to know all of these topics:

- Working with your organization
- Managing a pre-assigned project team
- Negotiating for project resources
- Acquiring project resources
- Relying on virtual project teams

Acquiring the Project Team

Negotiate and influence

Wrong resources affect project's success

Alternate resources
- Costs
- Competency
- Training
- Legal, regulatory, or mandatory criteria

ITTO: Acquire Project team

Inputs	Tools & Techniques	Outputs
Human resource management plan	Pre-assignment	Project staff assignments
Enterprise environmental factors	Negotiation	Resource calendars
Organizational process assets	Acquisition	Project management plan updates
	Virtual teams	
	Multi-criteria decision analysis	

Acquiring the Project Team

Pre-assignment

Negotiation

Acquisition

In order to complete a project the project manager needs something special – the project team! The project team is the collection of individuals that will actually be doing the work as defined in the project plan. They're the experts, the resources, and the roles that the project manager has to oversee and work with in order to get the project to its glorious finish.

So how does it work in your organization? Does the project team get assigned to the project manager or does the project manager get to cherry pick the project team members? Your organization's policies and procedures will likely outline how the project team is built, or inherited, by the project manager. Every organization is different, and the culture and organizational structure will influence how the project team is created. Certainly project priority, the project sponsor, and good old politics come into play when it comes to which project team member you're assigned or allowed to have on your project.

_____

_____

_____

_____

_____

_____

_____

Working with Virtual Teams

Geographically dispersed individuals

Experts in different geographical areas

Inclusion of workers from home offices

Project members with varying schedules

People with mobility handicaps

The deletion or reduction of travel expenses

Ideally, the project team is collocated – meaning the project team can work side-by-side with one another. A collocated project team communicates easier, can be more civil, and can move the project work along by joining efforts and creating synergy. Knowing that we don't live in an ideal world, however, collocated teams are falling prey to virtual teams. A virtual team is just a nice way of saying non-collocated. Individuals are dispersed around the globe and they rely on collaborative software, email, and telephones to communicate and work together.

Multi-Criteria Decision Analysis for Team

Availability

Costs

Experience

Ability

Knowledge

Skills

Attitude

International factors

Results of Team Acquisition

Project staff assignments

Resource calendars

Project management plan updates

LEAD PROJECT TEAM DEVELOPMENT

YOUR TEAM NEEDS TO WORK TOGETHER AND RELY ON ONE ANOTHER

The project team is developed by enhancing the competencies of the individual project team members and promoting the interaction of all the project team members. Throughout the project, the project manager will have to work to develop the project team. The project manager may have to develop an individual team member's skills so that she can complete her assignments. The project manager will also have to work to develop the project team as a whole so that the team can work together to complete the project. The project manager can use certain tools, techniques, and approaches to develop the project team. That's what this module details:

- Using general management skills
- Training the project team
- Using team building activities
- Establishing ground rules for the project team
- Working with non-collocated teams
- Establishing a rewards and recognition system
- Assessing the team performance

9.3 Develop Project Team

Process to improve competencies

Promote team member interaction

Enhance overall project performance

Overall goals of this process:
- Improve teamwork
- Motivate employees
- Reduce turnover rate
- Improve overall project performance

ITTO: Develop Project Team

Inputs	Tools & Techniques	Outputs
Human resource management plan	Interpersonal skills	Team performance assessments
Project staff assignments	Training	Enterprise environmental factors updates
Resource calendars	Team-building activities	
	Ground rules	
	Colocation	
	Recognition and rewards	
	Personnel assessment tools	

Leading Team Development

Interpersonal skills – soft skills
- Communication
- Emotional intelligence
- Conflict resolution
- Influence

Training the project team

Team building activities

Forming, storming, norming, performing, and adjourning

Regardless of the team's locale, the project manager can attempt to facilitate team development. Team development is a natural process that project teams cycle through as they learn about one another and accept their positions and roles within the project team. Technically, there are four stages of team development:

- Forming. The project team is coming together for the first time and pleasantries are offered. Um, obviously if the project team has worked together in the past forming doesn't take too long.
- Storming. Ooh – things are heating up. People on the team are exerting their influence, solidifying their positions, and trying to stake their leadership position within the project. This leadership can be for good or for bad.
- Norming. Alright, things have settled down and the project team has accepted their roles as leaders or followers.
- Performing. Here's the good part – the project team has accepted their roles and they're now focusing on completing the project work.

_____

_____

_____

_____

_____

_____

_____

Team Development, continued

Ground rules

Colocation – tight matrix

Recognition and rewards
- Money
- Throughout the project
- Avoid zero sum rewards

Personal assessment tools
- Attitudinal surveys
- Structured interviews

Team Performance Assessments

Improvements in skills

Team competency

Reduced staff turn over rate

Team cohesiveness

MANAGE THE PROJECT TEAM

MANAGING THE PROJECT TEAM TO GET PROJECT RESULTS

Now that the project manager has planned for the human resources and developed the project team, he can focus on managing the project team. This process involves tracking each team member's performance, offering feedback, taking care of project issues, and managing those pesky change requests that can affect the project team and its work. The staffing management plan may be updated based on lessons learned and changes within the team management process. The project manager will have to manage the project team. This includes:

- Observing and conversing with project team members
- Completing project team appraisals
- Resolving and managing team conflict
- Creating an issue log

9.4 Manage Project Team

Tracking team member performance

Offering feedback to team members

Managing team changes

Influencing team behavior

Resolving conflict

ITTO: Manage Project Team

Inputs	Tools & Techniques	Outputs
Human resource management plan	Observation and conversation	Change requests
Project staff assignments	Project performance appraisals	Project management plan updates
Team performance assessments	Conflict management	Project documents updates
Issue log	Interpersonal skills	Enterprise environmental factors updates
Work performance reports		Organizational process assets updates
Organizational process assets		

Utilizing Organizational Process Assets

Organizational process assets can help manage the project team:
- Certificates of appreciation
- Newsletters
- Project websites
- Bonus structures
- Corporate apparel

Conflict Management

Conflict is natural

Team issue

Openness resolves conflict

Focus on issues, not personalities

Focus on present, not past

Managing Conflict

Relative importance of the conflict

Time pressure for conflict resolution

Positions of each person involved

Motivation to resolve conflict for short-term or long-term

Solving Problems

Withdrawal (avoiding)

Smoothing (accommodating)

Compromising

Forcing

Collaborating

Problem solving (confronting)

- **Withdrawal.** Have you ever been talked to death by a proposed solution that caused you to give up and leave the conversation? You withdraw from the disagreement and just let the other person have their way, as it was easier than fighting over your proposed solution.
- **Smoothing.** Smoothing is when the commonalities are stressed and the differences are downplayed. Smoothing smooths the magnitude of the problem.
- **Compromising.** Compromising always sounds so nice but it really isn't. Compromising means that both parties have to give up something that they want. Both parties give up something, and that's why compromising is often called a lose-lose.
- **Forcing.** Forcing is when one party forces their will on the other party. The person with the power in the project or organization makes the decision.
- **Collaborating.** This is a win-win and is the same approach as problem solving.
- **Problem solving.** This approach is the most welcome and probably the most common in our projects. Problem solving is about finding a solution to the problem in a spirit of cooperation.

_____

_____

_____

_____

_____

_____

_____

Relying on Interpersonal Skills

Leadership – aligning, motivating, inspiring

Influencing – organizational structure and authority
- Persuasive
- Active and effective listening
- Aware of project team interactions and issues
- Maintaining trust while also managing the project team

Making Effective Decisions

Focus on project goals

Follow a decision-making process

Study environmental factors

Analyze information

Develop personal qualities of project team members

Stimulate team creativity

Manage risk

Be approachable

Management Styles

Autocratic: The project manager makes all decisions

Democratic: The project team is involved with the decisions

Laissez Faire: the project manager allows the team to lead and make decisions

Exceptional: the project manager manages by exception (reactive)

Five Project Management Powers

Expert - experienced

Reward - incentive

Formal - positional

Coercive - threatened

Referent – references

- **Expert.** The project team sees you, the project manager, as an expert in the technology or discipline the project focuses on. Makes sense, right? It's easier to trust and follow someone when they know what the heck they're talking about.
- **Reward.** The project team sees you as someone who can reward them for their work. Everyone's happy when they know the project manager can give bonuses, good reviews, and other rewards.
- **Formal.** The project team sees you a figure head without any real power. This weak power may also be known as positional power.
- **Coercive.** The project team sees you as someone who can punish them if they don't do their work on time and as expected. Coercive power can be useful when project team members don't respond to project incentives – it's the carrot or the stick mentality.
- **Referent.** The project team sees you as someone acting on someone else's behalf. For example, you say, "Team we're doing it this way because Marcy the CEO put me in charge." This works especially well when you actually have a CEO named Marcy.

Learning Game!

http://www.instructing.com/wp-content/pub/9/story.html

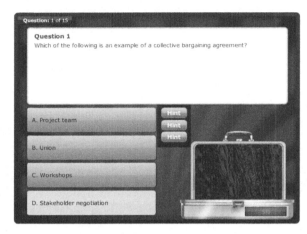

Chapter exam

PLAN PROJECT COMMUNICATIONS MANAGEMENT

COMMUNICATION IS 90% OF PROJECT MANAGEMENT

Communication planning is actually done very early in the project planning processes. It's essential to answer the previous questions as early as possible because their outcomes can affect the remainder of the project planning. Throughout the project, updates to communications planning are expected. Even the responses to the five project management communication questions can change as stakeholders, project team members, vendors, and other project interfaces change.. Communication is key to most of project management. This lecture defines:

- Examining the communications model
- Analyzing communication requirements
- Determining the communications technology
- Creating the Communications Management Plan

_____

_____

_____

_____

_____

_____

_____

_____

10.1 Plan Communications Management

Communication is paramount in project management

Creates project communications management plan

Defines how communication will be managed and controlled

Linked to stakeholder management and engagement

"The best years of your life are the ones in which you decide your problems are your own. You do not blame them on your mother, the ecology, or the president. You realize that you control your own destiny."

– Albert Ellis

ITTO: Plan Communications Management

Inputs	Tools & Techniques	Outputs
Project management plan	Communication requirements analysis	Communications management plan
Stakeholder register	Communication technology	Project documents updates
Enterprise environmental factors	Communication models	
Organizational process assets	Communication methods	
	Meetings	

Who are stakeholders?

Persons and organizations

Involved in the project

Affected positively or negatively by project

Some can exert influence over the project

Stakeholder Register

Identification information

Assessment information

Stakeholder classification

Project Communications Management Planning

Who needs what information?

Who is authorized to access the information?

Who will provide the information?

When do they need it?

What modality?

Where will the information be stored?

Will time zones, language barriers, or cross-cultural issues affect the communication?

Several factors affect project communications and how you'll communicate:

- Urgency of the information to be communicated. If your project has just turned disastrous is an email really the best way to communicate the information? The urgency of the information should dictate how the project manager communicates – and is expected by the stakeholders to communicate.
- Communication technologies. Web sites, email, instant messaging, text messages, and more – all technologies that help ease communication between the project manager, project team members, and other key stakeholders. It's a good idea, however, to identify the preferred methods for communicating at the launch of the project. You probably don't want status reports delivered via voice mail.
- Project staffing. Large projects, sometimes called macro projects, may have a dedicated administrative staff that can help ease the communication demands. Smaller projects, micro and MAC projects, likely don't have this luxury so communication demands fall onto the project manager and the project team.
- Project length and priority. Long-term, important projects need a defined schedule for how and when project communications will take place. It's essential for the project manager and the project team to document the communication expectations on larger and high-profile projects. A consistent schedule for communications is part of successful project management and keeps stakeholders abreast of the project's progress.
- Project environment. Some projects are loose, small, and even volunteer-driven. Other projects are important, dangerous, or expensive. The nature of the project will, to some extent, determine the type and frequency of project communications. The organization of the project team will also affect how communication will occur – consider a virtual team and its communication challenges compared to a collocated team working in a war room.

_____

_____

_____

Communications Channel Formula

N(N-1)/2

10(10-1)/2

90/2=45

How many more communication channels?

Activity: Consider that you have 340 stakeholders in your project this week. Next week you'll have 23 more stakeholders. How many more communication channels will you have next week compared to now?

_____

_____

_____

_____

_____

_____

_____

_____

Communication Requirements

Organization charts

Stakeholder responsibility relationships

Disciplines, departments, and specialties

Logistics of involvement

Internal and external communication needs

Stakeholder information

Communication Technology

Urgency of the need for information

Availability of technology

Ease of use

Project environment

Sensitivity and confidentiality of the information

Communication Model

Sender

Encoder

Medium

Decoder

Receiver

Noise

Barriers

Acknowledgements

Feedback/Response

Communication Methods

Interactive communication

Push communication

Pull communication

Communications Management Plan

Stakeholder communication requirements

Information to be communicated

Reason for the distribution

Time frame and frequency for the distribution

Person responsible for communicating the information

Person responsible for authorizing release of confidential information

A project management principle: 90 percent of project manager's time is spent communicating. Consider all of the project team members, management, other project managers, vendors, regulatory agencies, and other stakeholders the project manager has to communicate with in order for the project to be successful. This project management plan defines who needs what information, when do they need it, and in what modality. Part of the communications management plan is a schedule of expected communication types such as reports, interviews, and scheduled meetings.

Communications Management Plan

Methods or technologies

Resources allocated for communication activities

Escalation process

Method for updating and refining the communications management plan

Glossary of common terminology

Flow charts of the information flow in the project

Communication constraints

MANAGE PROJECT COMMUNICATIONS

MANAGING THE DAY-TO-DAY EFFORT OF THE PROJECT COMMUNICATIONS

Now that the project's communications management plan has been created, it's time to execute it. Managing project communications is the process of ensuring that the proper stakeholders get the appropriate information when and how they need it. Essentially, it's the implementation of the communications management plan. This plan details how the information is to be created and dispersed, and also how the dispersed information is archived. Managing project communications ensures that the right people, get the right message, at the right time, in the right modality.

- Examining communication skills
- Creating an Information Gathering and Retrieval System
- Dispersing project information
- Documenting the project's Lessons Learned
- Updating the organizational process assets

ITTO: Manage Communications

Following the communications management plan to:
- Create
- Collect
- Store
- Distribute
- Retrieve

Ensures flow of communication among project stakeholders

ITTO: Manage Communications

Inputs	Tools & Techniques	Outputs
Communications management plan	Communication technology	Project communications
		Project management plan updates
Work performance reports	Communication models	
Enterprise environmental factors	Communication methods	Project documents updates
Organizational process assets	Information management systems	Organizational process assets updates
	Performance reporting	

Information Distribution Techniques

Sender-receiver models

Choice of media

Writing style

Meeting management techniques

Facilitation techniques

Using an Information Management System

Hard copy documents: memos, letters, reports, press releases

Electronic communications: email, fax, voice, video and web conferences, websites, web publishing

Electronic project management tools: web software, project management software, virtual office support, collaborative tools

All of the project communications – okay, not all of it, but most of it – should be organized in a project communication retrieval system. This can be a fancy-schmancy database or just a well-organized banker's box. The reports, presentations, emails, stakeholder feedback, and other communiqué all will become part of the project's historical information and that can support the project's product once it goes into operations, as well as help other project managers learn from the current project.

_____

_____

_____

_____

_____

_____

_____

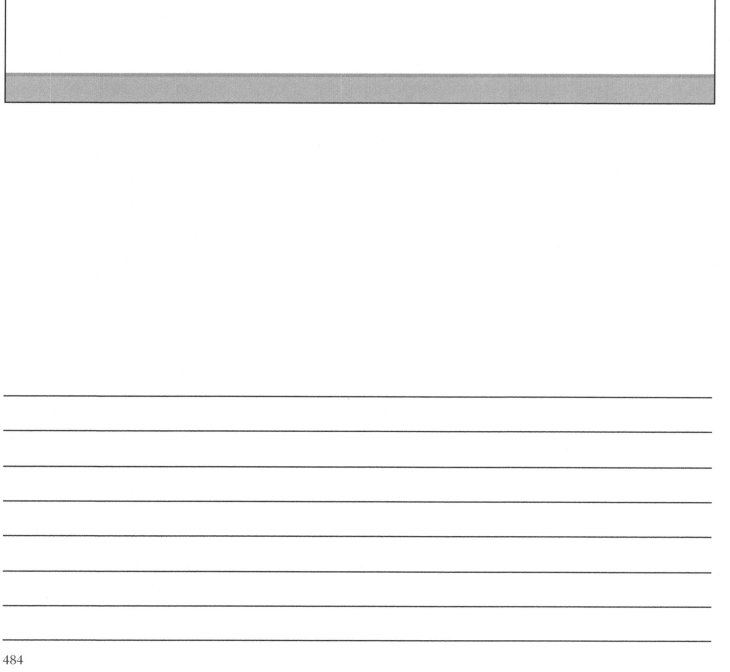

Performance Reports

Prior to project meetings

Forecasting
- Estimate to Complete
- Estimate at Completion

Analogy to other projects (benchmarking)

Work re-estimation

External events impact

Results of Information Distribution

Stakeholder notifications

Project reports

Project presentations

Project records

Feedback from stakeholders

Lessons learned

CONTROL PROJECT COMMUNICATIONS

ENSURING THAT THE PROJECT COMMUNICATIONS MANAGEMENT PLAN IS FOLLOWED

Throughout the project, customers and other stakeholders are going to need updates on the project performance, work status, and project information. The work performance information—the status of what's been completed and what's left to do—is always at the heart of performance reporting. Stakeholders want to be kept abreast of how the project is performing, but also what issues, risks, and conditions in the project have evolved.

Controlling communication is the process of following the communications management plan, distributing information, and sharing how the project is performing. Performance reporting is the process of collecting, organizing, and disseminating information on how project resources are being used to complete the project objectives. In other words, the people footing the bill and who are affected by the outcome of the project need some confirmation that things are going the way the project manager has promised. This lecture details:

- Determining the communication method
- Dispersing project information
- Creating an Issue Log

10.3 Control Communications

Right information, right parties, at the right time

Follows and enforces communications management plan

Ensures optimal information flow among the parties

ITTO: Control Communications

Inputs	Tools & Techniques	Outputs
Project management plan	Information management systems	Work performance information
Project communications	Expert judgment	Change requests
Issue log	Meetings	Project management plan updates
Work performance data		Project documents updates
Organizational process assets		Organizational process assets updates

Controlling Communications

Information management systems

Relying on expert judgment
- Leaders in the organization
- Consultants
- Subject matter experts
- PMO

Meetings

Performance Reports

Status reports

Progress measurements

Forecasts

Baseline to actual comparisons

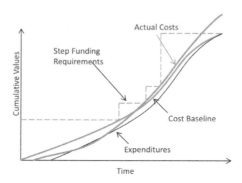

Forecasting Methods

Time series method
- Earned value
- Moving average
- Extrapolation
- Liner prediction
- Trend estimation
- Growth curve

Judgmental methods
- Intuitive judgments
- Opinions
- Probability

Forecasting Methods

Casual/econometric methods
- Causal factors for experiences
- Linear regression
- Autoregressive moving average (ARMA)
- Econometrics

Other methods...
- Simulation
- Probabilistic forecasting
- Ensemble forecasting

Learning Game!

http://www.instructing.com/wp-content/pub/10/story.html

Chapter exam

_____

_____

_____

_____

_____

_____

_____

_____

PLAN PROJECT RISK MANAGEMENT

PLANNING, ANALYZING, RESPONDING TO, AND CONTROLLING PROJECT RISKS

Risk management planning is not the identification of risks or even the response to known risks within a project. Risk management planning is how the project management team will complete the risk management activities within the project. These activities really set up the project to effectively manage the five other risk management activities. Risk management planning creates the risk management plan.

By deciding the approach to each of the risk management activities before moving into them, the project management team can more effectively identify risks, complete risk analysis, and then plan risk responses. In addition, planning for risk management also allows the project management team to create a strategy for the ongoing identification and monitoring of existing risks within the project. This lecture will define all of risk management planning:

- Defining project risk
- Hosting a risk planning meeting
- Creating a Risk Management Plan

What is risk?

Risk and reward

Risk is not always bad

Business risks

Pure risks

Planning for Risk Management

Risk appetite

Risk tolerance

Risk threshold

Stakeholder tolerance

Utility function

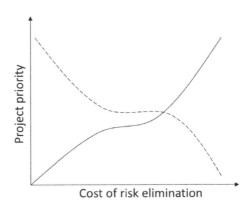

11.1 Plan Risk Management

Defines how risk management activities will occur

Risk activities in relation to project importance

Defines how the key stakeholders will:
- Identify risks
- Analyze risks
- Create risk responses
- Control risks

This subsidiary plan defines the process for risk management – how the risk management processes will take place within the project. It identifies the risks within the project, the process to record and rank those risks, and what the proposed risk responses may be.

_____

_____

_____

_____

_____

_____

_____

ITTO: Plan Risk Management

Inputs	Tools & Techniques	Outputs
Project management plan	Analytical techniques	Risk management plan
Project charter	Expert judgment	
Stakeholder register	Meetings	
Enterprise environmental factors		
Organizational process assets		

Planning Meetings and Analysis

Project manager, project team, stakeholders

Cost elements

Schedule activities

Risk management plan

"You don't have to see the whole staircase, just take the first step."

– Martin Luther King, Jr.

Relying on Risk Management Policies

Enterprise environmental factors

Nature of the work

Industry standards

Regulated policies

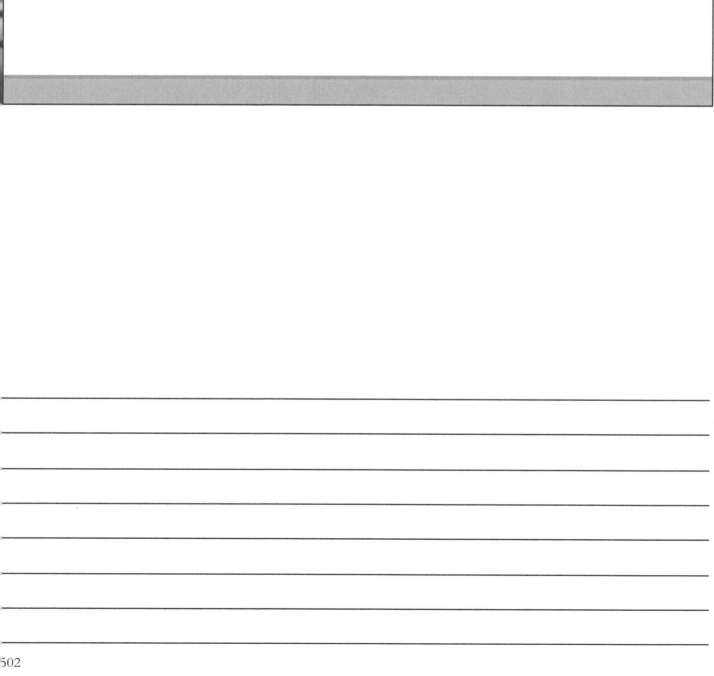

Creating a Risk Management Plan

Methodology

Roles and responsibilities

Budgeting

Timing

Risk categories

Creating a Risk Management Plan

Definitions of risk probability and impact

Probability and impact matrix

Stakeholder tolerances

Reporting formats

Tracking

IDENTIFY PROJECT RISK

ALWAYS BE ON THE LOOKOUT FOR NEW RISK EVENTS – FROM START TO FINISH

Risk identification is the systematic process of combing through the project, the project plan, the work breakdown structure (WBS), and all supporting documentation to identify as many of the risks that may affect the project as possible. Remember, a risk is an uncertain event or condition that may affect the project outcome. Risks can be positive or negative. This lecture includes:

- Reviewing project documentation
- Identifying the project risks
- Analyzing the project assumptions
- Diagramming project risks

Risk Categories

Risk Breakdown Structure

Technical, quality, or performance risks

Project management risks

Organization risks

External risks

11.2 Identify Risks

Identifying and documenting risks

Creates a risk register

Ongoing activity throughout the project

ITTO: Identify Risks

Inputs	Tools & Techniques	Outputs
Risk management plan	Documentation reviews	Risk register
Cost management plan	Information gathering techniques	
Schedule management plan	Checklist analysis	
Quality management plan	Assumptions analysis	
Human resource management plan	Diagramming techniques	
Scope baseline	SWOT analysis	
Activity cost estimates	Expert judgment	
Activity duration estimates		
Stakeholder register		
Project documents		
Procurement documents		
Enterprise environmental factors		
Organizational process assets		

Information Gathering Techniques

Brainstorming

Delphi Technique

Checklists

Assumptions analysis

Diagramming Techniques

SWOT

Expert judgment

Creating a Risk Register

Central risk repository

Identified risks

Potential responses

Root cause

Risk categories

Risk status

Recall that the risk register is a component of risk management – it's a database of the identified risks within the project and their probability, impact, and potential responses. The risk register should also identify the risk status, the outcome of past risk events, and the risk owners within the project. The register may also record triggers and thresholds and any other related information.

PERFORM PROJECT RISK ANALYSIS

ANALYZING THE RISK EVENTS FOR PROBABILITY AND IMPACT ON PROJECT SUCCESS

11.3 Perform Qualitative Risk Analysis

Fast, subjective approach to analysis

Qualify the risk for more analysis

Can be done as risks are identified

Cardinal or ordinal scale

The first, and somewhat shallow, risk analysis is qualitative analysis. Qualitative risk analysis "qualifies" the risks that have been identified in the project. Specifically, qualitative risk analysis examines and prioritizes the risks based on their probability of occurring and the impact on the project if the risks do occur. Qualitative risk analysis is a broad approach to ranking risks by priority, which then guides the risk reaction process. The end result of qualitative risk analysis (once risks have been identified and prioritized) can either lead to more in-depth quantitative risk analysis or move directly into risk response planning. Qualitative risk analysis is a high-level, fast method of qualifying the risk for more analysis. This lecture will define:

- Using a risk register
- Creating a risk probability and impact matrix
- Examining the data quality
- Categorizing risks
- Updating the risk register

ITTO: Perform Qualitative Risk Analysis

Inputs	Tools & Techniques	Outputs
Risk management plan	Risk probability and impact assessment	Project documents updates
Scope baseline	Probability and impact matrix	
Risk register	Risk data quality assessment	
Enterprise environmental factors	Risk categorization	
Organizational process assets	Risk urgency assessment	
	Expert judgment	

Probability-Impact Matrix

Odds and Impact

Risk	Probability	Impact	Risk Score
Data loss	Low	High	Moderate
Network speed	Moderate	Moderate	Moderate
Server downtime	High	Low	Moderate
Email service down	Low	Low	Low

Each identified risk

Subjective score

You can use red, amber, green, (sometimes called RAG rating), very low to very high, or do what I did in the example and just use low to high. See how it's subjective? Some risks will be obviously low impact and/or low probability while other risks will warrant a more heated discussion among the participants that are doing the qualitative analysis. The result of qualitative analysis is to "qualify" the more probable and more serious risks for additional analysis. This doesn't mean that you get to dismiss the risk events which are scored as low. All risks, including the low risks, are entered into a risk register, a database of all the risks within the project. The conditions and status are monitored as the project moves into execution.

Other Qualitative Tools

Risk Data Quality Assessment

Risk Categorization

Risk Urgency Assessment

Expert judgment

11.4 Perform Quantitative Risk Analysis

Quantifying the identified risks

Usually for the more serious risks
- Probability
- Impact

Helps with decision-making for risk response

ITTO: Perform Quantitative Risk Analysis

Inputs	Tools & Techniques	Outputs
Risk management plan	Data gathering and representation techniques	Project documents updates
Cost management plan	Quantitative risk analysis and modeling techniques	
Schedule management plan	Expert judgment	
Risk register		
Enterprise environmental factors		
Organizational process assets		

Quantitative risk analysis attempts to numerically assess the probability and impact of the identified risks. It also creates an overall risk score for the project. This method is more in-depth than qualitative risk analysis and relies on several different tools to accomplish its goal.

Qualitative risk analysis typically precedes quantitative risk analysis. I like to say that qualitative analysis qualifies risks, while quantitative analysis quantifies risks. All or a portion of the identified risks in qualitative risk analysis can be examined in the quantitative analysis. The performing organization may have policies on the risk scores in qualitative analysis that require the risks to advance to the quantitative analysis. The availability of time and budget may also be a factor in determining which risks should pass through quantitative analysis. Quantitative analysis is a more time-consuming process, and is, therefore, also more expensive. This lecture will cover:

* Gathering risk data
* Creating a risk probability distribution
* Modeling risk data
* Creating a contingency reserve
* Updating the risk register

Goals of Quantitative Analysis

Likelihood of reaching project success

Likelihood of reaching a project objective

Project's risk exposure

Contingency reserve

Identify the risks with the largest impact

Determine realistic time, cost, and scope targets

Performing Quantitative Analysis

Interviewing stakeholders and experts

Risk distributions

Sensitivity analysis

Expected Monetary Value

Modeling and simulation

Expert judgment

Quantitative analysis aims to quantify the risk exposure and often ties a dollar amount to the risk event. The process of quantitative risk analysis isn't as quick or nearly as subjective as qualitative risk analysis. The project manager, project team members, risk specialists, and business analysts will take the identified risks and complete testing, business cases, root cause analysis, and other studies in their attempt to quantify the risks.

Using Sensitivity Analysis

Identifies the risks with most potential impact on the project

Measures and examines uncertainties

Tornado diagram often used with sensitivity analysis

Probability-Impact Matrix

Cardinal scale

Risk exposure

Sum of contingency reserve

"Hedging bets"

Probability-Impact Matrix

Risk event	Probability	Impact	Ex$V
A	.60	-10,000	-6,000
B	.20	-75,000	-15,000
C	.10	25,000	2,500
D	.40	-85,000	-34,000

Contingency reserve = $52,500

Examining the Results of Quantitative Risk Analysis

Probabilistic analysis of the project

Probability of achieving time and cost objectives

Prioritized list of quantified risks

Trends in quantitative risk analysis results

CREATE PROJECT RISK RESPONSES

THERE ARE SEVEN RISK RESPONSES FOR
RISK EVENTS WITHIN A PROJECT

Risk response planning is all about options and actions. It focuses on how to decrease the possibility of risks adversely affecting the project's objectives and also on how to increase the likelihood of positive risks that can aid the project. Risk response planning assigns responsibilities to people and groups close to the risk event. Risks will increase or decrease based on the effectiveness of risk response planning. This lecture will help you learn everything there is to know for your PMP exam about risk responses. This includes:

- Determining the risk tolerance
- Considering negative risks
- Planning for positive risks
- Accepting risk responses
- Creating a contingent response strategy

11.5 Plan Risk Responses

Enhance opportunities

Reduce risks

Documents risk responses

Tracks outcomes for lessons learned

ITTO: Plan Risk Responses

Inputs	Tools & Techniques	Outputs
Risk management plan	Strategies for negative risks or threats	Project management plan updates
Risk register	Strategies for positive risks or opportunities	Project documents updates
	Contingent response strategies	
	Expert judgment	

Responding to Negative Risks

Avoidance

Transference

Mitigation

- Mitigation. This is an action to reduce or eliminate the risk event, its probability, and/or impact. You'll likely use mitigation when you've identified a risk event that has a high impact on the project. In some instances you can spend monies to reduce the risk's likelihood of occurring or you might allot additional time or change the project network diagram to mitigate the risk event.
- Transference. You've probably used transference already by hiring someone else to own the risk event. Consider a construction project: the electrical work is too dangerous for an organization to do on their own, so they hire a licensed electrician to complete the dangerous electrical work. The risk of electricity didn't disappear. It's still dangerous, but the electrician owns the work. Transference usually requires a contract between the two parties and a payment from the project to the new risk owner.
- Avoidance. This one is easy – you're taking measures to avoid the risk. Let's say you're managing a database conversion project. One of the risk events is the loss of data if the conversion takes place during the usual Monday through Friday work week. You avoid the risk by doing the conversion outside of the usual business hours – nights and weekends.

Managing Positive Risks

Exploiting

Sharing

Enhancing

- Enhance. This risk response is an effort to make a positive risk event happen. Your project can earn $25,000 in bonuses if your project team doesn't have to work overtime. In order to enhance the positive risk event you hire a contractor for $5,000 to help the project team complete their assignments on time. You've enhanced the positive risk by spending $5,000.
- Exploit. Wouldn't you take advantage of a great positive risk? Let's say your project creates a by-product, such as data or raw materials, that can be sold on the marketplace. You'd work to exploit this risk to sell the by-product and realize an unexpected, but welcome, profit.
- Share. Sharing is nice. A vendor will give your project a steep discount on their software if you'll purchase 100 licenses. Your project only needs 70 licenses so you identify other project managers and business units that could use the product and take advantage of the offered discount.

Managing Positive and Negative Risks

Acceptance
- Laws
- Constraints
- Discounts
- Weather
- Force Majeure

- Acceptance. Sometimes a risk event is so tiny that you just accept the risk and move along. Other times, however, there's nothing you can do about the risk regardless of its probability and impact so you just accept it – like a pending law, company policy, or weather.

Contingent Responses

When certain events occur

Certain predefined conditions

Triggers

Risk registers

Risk Register Updates

Risks, owners, responsibilities

Response strategies

Triggers, warning signs, conditions

Contingency plans

Fallback plans

Managing Risks

Residual risks

Secondary risks

Risk response contracts

Justifying risk reduction

CONTROL PROJECT RISK

CONTROLLING PROJECT RISKS TO MINIMIZE THREATS AND MAXIMIZE OPPORTUNITIES

Risks must be actively monitored, and new risks must be responded to as they are discovered. Risk monitoring and control is the process of monitoring identified risks for signs that they may be occurring, controlling identified risks with the agreed-upon responses, and looking for new risks that may creep into the project. Risk monitoring and control also is concerned with the documentation of the success or failure of risk response plans and keeping records of metrics that signal risks are occurring or disappearing from the project. This lecture will help you to:

- Reassess the project for risks
- Complete a risk audit
- Examine the project trends and technical performance
- Host a project status meeting
- Recommend corrective and preventive actions

Control Risks

Implementing risk response plans

Tracking identified risks

Monitoring residual risks

Evaluating risk process effectiveness

You've several activities to do with the project team when it comes to risk management:

- When risk events are happening in the project and your project team fires away with the planned risk responses, you have to check that the risk responses are working as you planned. If not, you'll need fast-action to find a new solution to squelch the risk.
- Determine if the project assumptions are proving false and if they're becoming project risks. Assumptions are anything that you believe to be true, but you've not proven to be true. If your assumptions prove false then they're becoming risks in the project.
- Monitor risk thresholds and your risk triggers. This means as part of managing the project team you're communicating pending risk events and what risks could be coming into play.
- Encourage the project team to be identifying new risk events or risk events that haven't been identified as the project work happens. This process provides time to perform qualitative and quantitative analysis and to create risk responses. Of course, all newly-discovered risk events are also recorded in the risk register.

_____

_____

_____

_____

_____

_____

_____

ITTO: Control Risks

Inputs	Tools & Techniques	Outputs
Project management plan	Risk reassessment	Work performance information
Risk register	Risk audits	Change requests
Work performance data	Variance and trend analysis	Project management plan updates
Work performance reports	Technical performance measurement	Project documents updates
	Reserve analysis	Organizational process assets updates
	Meetings	

Risk Monitoring and Control

Risk reassessment

Risk audits

Variance and trend analysis

Technical performance information

Reserve analysis

Status meetings

"Success is not final, failure is not fatal: it is the courage to continue that counts."

— Winston Churchill

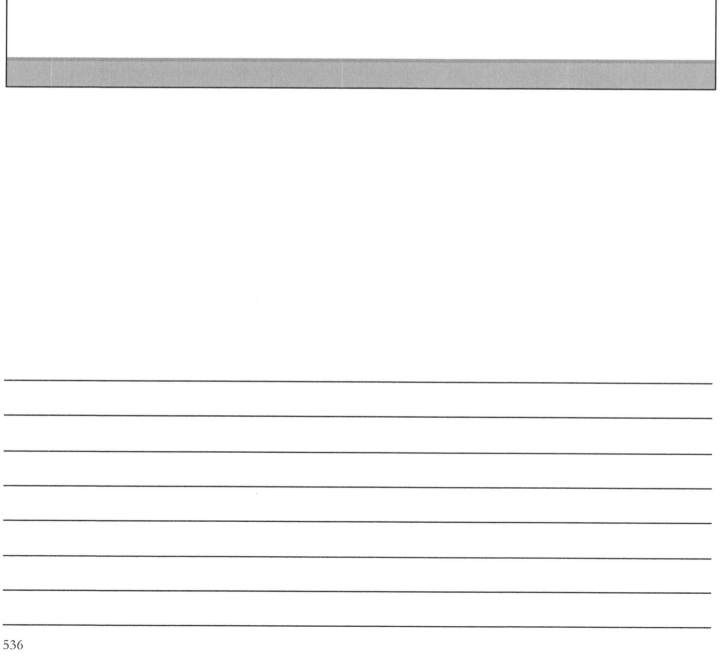

Results of Monitoring and Control

Work performance information

Change requests
- ◦ Corrective actions
- ◦ Preventive actions

Project management plan updates

Project document updates

Organizational process assets

Learning Game!

http://www.instructing.com/wp-content/pub/11/story.html

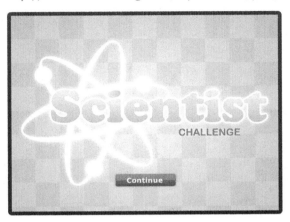

Chapter exam

PLAN PROJECT PROCUREMENT MANAGEMENT

PLANNING FOR PROCUREMENT, WORKING WITH CONTRACTS, CONTROLLING PROCUREMENT ACTIVITIES, AND CLOSING OUT PROCUREMENT

Procurement planning is the process of identifying which part of the project should be procured from resources outside of the organization. Generally, procurement decisions are made early on in the planning processes. Procurement planning centers on four elements:

- Whether procurement is needed
- What to procure
- How much to procure
- When to procure

12.1 Plan Procurement Management

Documents the procurement approach

Defines the procurement decisions

Identifies potential sellers

Approach for acquiring resources and services

ITTO: Plan Procurement Management

Inputs	Tools & Techniques	Outputs
Project management plan	Make-or-buy analysis	Procurement management plan
Requirements documentation	Expert judgment	Procurement statement of work
Risk register	Market research	Procurement documents
Activity resource requirements	Meetings	Source selection criteria
Project schedule		Make-or-buy decisions
Activity cost estimates		Change requests
Stakeholder register		Project documents updates
Enterprise environmental factors		
Organizational process assets		

Procurement Management Plan

Type of contracts to be used

Risk management issues

Independent estimates

Organizational procurement procedures

Procurement documents

Managing multiple suppliers

Procurement Management Plan

Coordinating procurement activities

Constraints and assumptions

Required procurement lead time

Make or buy decisions

Scheduling deliverables in the contract

Performance bonds, insurance

Procurement Management Plan

WBS provided by seller

Form and format for SOW documents

Identifying pre-qualified sellers

Procurement metrics for evaluations

Source Selection Criteria

Understanding of need

Life cycle cost

Technical capability

Risk

Management approach

Technical approach

Warranty

Financial capacity

Production capacity and interest

Business size and type

Past performance of sellers

References

Intellectual property rights

Proprietary rights

Procurement Overview

Buyer is a stakeholder for seller

Seller is the project management team

Terms and conditions of contract for seller

External and internal "contracts"

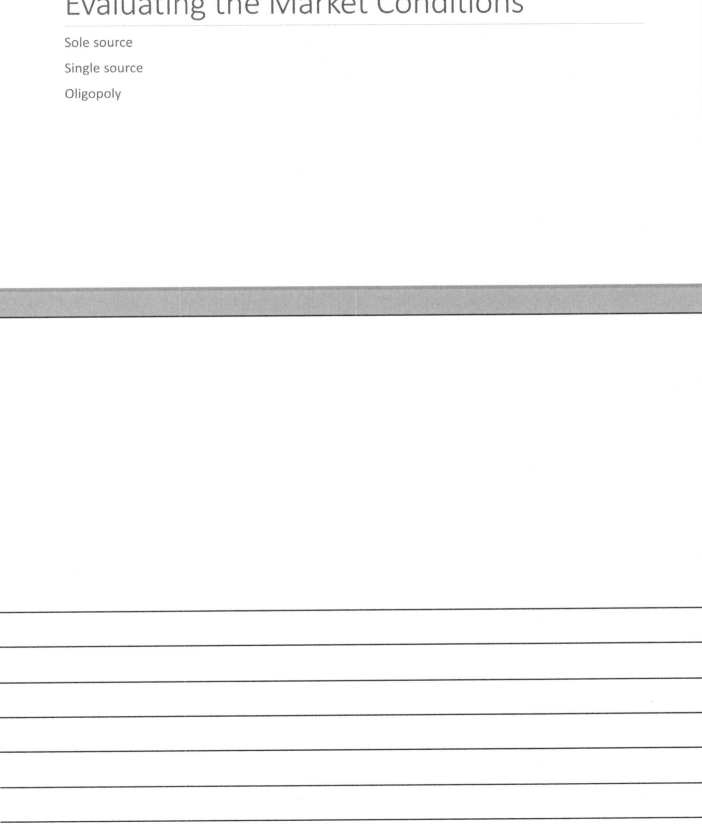

Evaluating the Market Conditions

Sole source

Single source

Oligopoly

REVIEW PROJECT PROCUREMENT CONTRACTS

KNOW THESE CONTRACT TYPES AND THEIR CHARACTERISTICS FOR THE PMP EXAM

There are multiple types of contracts when it comes to procurement. The project work, the market, and the nature of the purchase determine the contract type. Here are some general rules that CAPM and PMP exam candidates, and project managers, should know:

- A contract is a formal agreement between the buyer and the seller. Contracts can be oral or written—although written is preferred.
- The United States backs all contracts through the court system.
- Contracts should clearly state all requirements for product acceptance.
- Any changes to the contract must be formally approved, controlled, and documented.
- A contract is not fulfilled until all of its requirements are met.
- Contracts can be used as a risk mitigation tool, as in transferring the risk. All contracts have some level of risk; depending on the contract type, the risk can be transferred to the seller. If a risk response strategy is to transfer, risks associated with procurement are considered secondary risks and must go through the risk management process.

All About Contracts

A contract is a formal agreement

The United States backs all contracts through the court system

Contracts state all requirements for product acceptance

Changes to the contract must be formally approved, controlled, and documented

Contracts can be used as a risk mitigation tool

Most projects work with vendors for contracted labor, materials, or services. Whenever a project has to deal with an entity outside of the immediate performing organization a contract is needed. A contract is a legally-binding document that is backed up by the court system (in the United States). A contract defines the offer and consideration – an amount of money in consideration for the work or services provided by the vendor.

Contract Legalities

Fixed Price or Cost Reimbursable

Contain an offer

Have been accepted

Provide for a consideration (payment)

Be for a legal purpose

Be executed by someone with capacity and authority

Firm Fixed-Price Contracts (FFP)

Most common contract

Seller carries risk of cost overruns

Buyer specifies what's to be purchased

Changes to the scope

This contract type, also known as a lump-sum contract, defines a price for the contracted work regardless of the materials or labor used. For example, if you hired a contractor to add a deck onto your house you might use a fixed-priced contract where the cost of the deck is $7,500 – that's the most you'll pay for the deck. The vendor has the risk should there be overtime in labor, wasted materials by his crew, or if the cost of materials fluctuates. You, however, will only pay $7,500 for the work.

Fixed-Price Incentive Fee Contracts (FPIF)

Financial incentives for performance

Cost, schedule, technical performance

Price ceiling

Seller carries risk of overruns

This contract type is similar to a fixed-price contract but you and the vendor have worked out some details on a bonus structure. For example, if you were remodeling a building into condos you might have milestone dates within the schedule that represent bonuses to the vendor if he can meet them. The incentive for the vendor is the bonus pay, the incentive for you, the buyer, is that you'll get to rent or sell your condos as soon as the vendor gets the work done. There are several models of fixed-price incentive fee contracts including penalties for a vendor missing deadlines.

Fixed Price with Economic Price Adjustment Contracts (FP-EPA)

Long-term contracts

Pre-defined financial adjustments

Inflation, cost increases, decreases

External conditions

Cost Reimbursable Overview

Cost plus a fee

Scope of work can't be defined early

High risks may exists in the project

Buyer carries risk of overruns

Cost-plus contracts are generally riskiest to you, the buyer. These contracts charge the buyer for contracted work plus a variable such as time fees, materials, or the worst – a percentage of the costs associated with the work. These contracts give the vendor lots of room to waste materials and charge you for their mistakes. These are the riskiest contract types for buyers. Above all avoid the dreaded cost plus a percentage of cost contract. The vendor can actually increase their profit margin by wasting materials. Not good.

Cost Plus Fixed Fee Contracts (CPFF)

All allowable costs

Fixed fee of the initial estimated costs

Fee paid for completed work

Fee is constant unless scope changes

Cost Plus Incentive Fee (CPIF)

All allowable costs

Fee based on performance goals

Incentive sharing (often 80/20)

Contract defines measurements

Cost Plus Award Fee Contract (CPAF)

All allowable costs

Performance criteria for fee to seller

Subjective review by buyer

Award is determined by the buyer

Time and Materials Contract (T&M)

Seller is paid an hourly fee

Seller is paid for materials

Not-to-exceed clause

Time limits for contract

"If I had eight hours to chop down a tree, I'd spend six hours sharpening my ax."

– Abraham Lincoln

DECIDE TO BUILD OR TO BUY IN PROJECTS

A MATHEMATICAL ANALYSIS OF BUYING OR BUILDING A PROJECT SOLUTION

Reasons to Buy or Build

Less costly

Use in-house skills

Control of work

Control of intellectual property

Learn new skills

Available staff

Focus on core project work

Build v. Buy Decisions

| Build $65,000 | Buy $52,000 | Difference Buy v. Build $13,000 |

| Build Monthly Fees $8,500 | Buy Monthly Fees $10,500 | Difference Monthly Fees $2,000 |

Divide Differences
$13,000/$2,000 = 6.5 months

PRACTICE ACTIVITY

PRACTICE THE BUY OR BUILD DETERMINATION

Determine to Build or Buy

Your team can create a solution for $245,600 and it will cost $23,500 per month to support. A vendor promises that you can purchase their solution for $12,000, but you'll have a monthly fee of $49,000. When could your solution be a better financial decision than the vendor's offer?

Build	Buy	Difference Buy v. Build

Build Monthly Fees	Buy Monthly Fees	Difference Monthly Fees

Divide Differences

Answer: Determine to Build or Buy

Your team can create a solution for $245,600 and it will cost $23,500 per month to support. A vendor promises that you can purchase their solution for $12,000, but you'll have a monthly fee of $49,000. When could your solution be a better financial decision than the vendor's offer?

Build $245,600	Buy $23,500	Difference Buy v. Build $222,100
Build Monthly Fees $23,500	Buy Monthly Fees $49,000	Difference Monthly Fees 25,500

Divide Differences
$221,100/$25,500 = 8.7 months

EXECUTE THE PROJECT PROCUREMENT MANAGEMENT PLAN

PROCURING GOODS AND SERVICES FOR THE PROJECT

Conducting project procurement means that your determining which vendor to hire for your project. Once the plan-contracting process has been completed, the actual process of asking the sellers to participate can begin. Fortunately, the sellers, not the buyers, perform most of the activity in this process—usually at no additional cost to the project.

This lecture will help you to understand these topics:

- Hosting a bidders conference
- Advertising for bidders
- Developing a qualified sellers list
- Creating a Procurement Document Package
- Using a weighting system
- Working with independent estimates
- Creating a screening system
- Negotiating for the best deal
- Relying on seller rating systems

12.2 Conduct Procurements

Obtaining seller responses

Selecting the seller

Award a contract

Vendors need the SOW and may get it one of several ways.
- Preferred vendors list. Most organizations have a preferred vendors list that they'll issue the SOW to.
- Advertising. Government agencies typically are required to announce projects that are open for bid in the local newspapers. SOWs are issued to qualified vendors that will participate in the bidding process.
- Evaluation criteria. An organization may evaluate potential vendors to determine if the vendors qualify to participate in the procurement process. For example, an evaluation criteria could be top-secret security clearance with two certified Project Management Professionals on staff.

ITTO: Conduct Procurements

Inputs	Tools & Techniques	Outputs
Procurement management plan	Bidder conference	Selected sellers
Procurement documents	Proposal evaluation techniques	Agreements
Source selection criteria	Independent estimates	Resource calendars
Seller proposals	Expert judgment	Change requests
Project documents	Advertising	Project management plan updates
Make-or-buy decisions	Analytical techniques	Project documents updates
Procurement statement of work	Procurement negotiations	
Organizational process assets		

Procurement Details

Qualified seller lists

Bidder conferences

Advertising

SOW updates

In the planning process group you created the procurement management plan. Now you're about to execute this beauty of a plan by inviting sellers to bid on your project work. Once you've collected the bids and proposals then you'll choose the best vendor for your project. Recall that the procurement management plan defined the acceptable contract types and the processes of how you'll choose vendors. Some of the information I share in this section might not apply to you at all as your organization may manage the procurement process away from the project managers. Don't sweat it – managing a project is tricky enough, let someone else deal with the vendors.

From the Buyer

SOW

Request for Quote

Invitation for Bid

Request for Proposal

Request for Information

- Request for Quote (RFQ) – A RFQ is a document that asks the sellers to provide a price for the services or goods the organization is interested in purchasing. An RFQ means the buyer wants to purchase, but is interested in price only.
- Invitation for Bid (IFB) – Like an RFQ, an IFB is a document from the buyer to the sellers asking for a price only. It's, for essential purposes, the same type of document as an RFQ.
- Request for Proposal (RFP) – A RFP is document from the buyer to the sellers asking for a proposed solution and a price. This document is different than the IFB and the RFQ, because the buyer is inviting the vendor to create a solution for the project. Proposals are generally more work for the vendor, because the vendor may create a solution for the buyer but they still may not be awarded the contract.

From the Seller

Quote

Bid

Information

Proposal

Seller Selection

Weighting system

Independent estimates

Screening systems

Contract negotiation

Seller rating systems

Expert judgment

Proposal evaluation

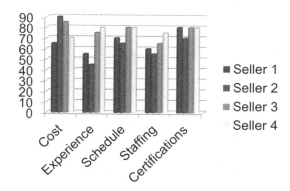

The buyer then evaluate the bids, quotes, and proposals to determine which vendor can best answer the project's needs. Organizational policies may dictate how a vendor gets selected, but most organizations choose a vendor based on one or more of the following:

- Weighted system. Categories are identified, such as cost, time, experience, references, and points are assigned to each category. Each vendor's bid, quote, or proposal is measured and scored in each of these categories. The vendor that receives the highest score is awarded the contract.

- Independent estimates. This approach is also called a "should-cost" estimate. The buyer hires a third-party to create an estimate for the project's procured work. This third-party estimate serves as a means for the project work to be procured – as a guide to what the work "should cost."

- Screening systems. This popular approach identifies qualifications and specifications the proposed vendors must have in order to qualify for the project. If the vendor doesn't have these qualifications they're screened from the selection process.

- Negotiation. Negotiation is the process of the buyer and the seller giving and taking components of the work, the deliverables, the pay, and the schedule to reach an agreeable conclusion for both parties. Negotiations are often handled by a buyer's agent or purchasing agent on behalf of the project manager.

- Seller rating systems. Many organizations utilize a seller rating system. This is a database where project managers can rate their experience with vendors they've utilized in the past. Other project managers can use the database as a precursor to negotiations and awarding the project contract.

Procurement process

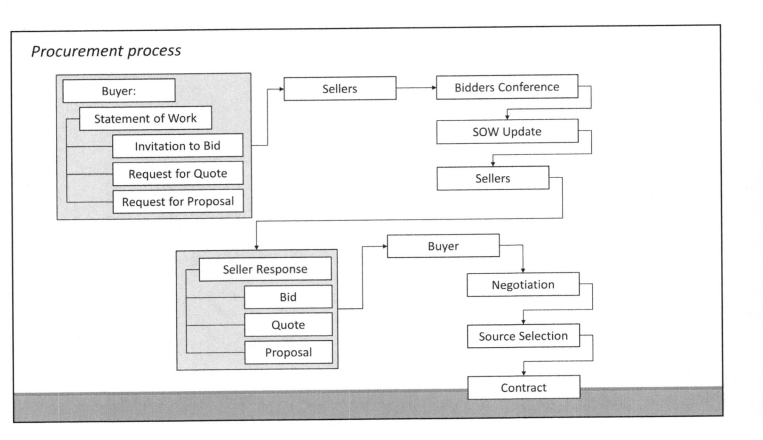

Contract Details (Agreement)

- SOW and/or deliverables
- Schedule baseline
- Performance reporting
- Period of performance
- Roles and Responsibilities
- Where work is to occur
- Pricing
- Payment terms
- Inspection and acceptance criteria
- Warranty

- Product support
- Limitation of liability
- Fees and retainage
- Penalties
- Incentives
- Insurance and performance bonds
- Subordinate subcontractor approvals
- Change request handling
- Termination/alternative dispute resolution

CONTROL PROJECT PROCUREMENT

BOTH PARTIES MUST ABIDE BY THE TERMS OF THE CONTRACT

Controlling procurements is the process of ensuring that both the buyer and the seller live up to the agreements in the contract. The project manager and the contract administrator must work together to make certain the seller meets its obligations, just as the vendor will ensure that the buyer lives up to its agreements as well. If either party does not fulfill its contractual requirements, legal remedies may ultimately be pursued.

A deal is a deal and this lecture will the project manager ensure that both parties, the buyer and the seller, live up to the terms of the contract.

- Creating a contract change control system
- Completing a performance review
- Paying the vendor
- Managing claims
- Creating a records management system

12.3 Control Procurements

Managing procurement relationships

Monitoring contract performance

Making changes and corrections to contract as needed

You could be the buyer or seller on the exam…

ITTO: Control Procurements

Inputs	Tools & Techniques	Outputs
Project management plan	Contract change control system	Work performance information
Procurement documents	Procurement performance reviews	Change requests
Agreements	Inspections and audits	Project management plan updates
Approved change requests	Payment systems	Project documents updates
Work performance reports	Claims administration	Organizational process assets updates
Work performance data	Records management system	
	Performance reporting	

Procurement and Processes

Direct and manage project execution

Report performance

Perform quality control

Perform integrated change control

Monitor and control risks

Once the buyer and the seller have reached an agreement a contract is entered into by both parties. A contract is a legally-binding agreement between the two parties and is backed by the United States court system. Both parties are expected to live up to their agreement, otherwise claims, mediation, or even arbitration ensues. Most contracts have provisions for how issues are escalated and if necessary into what court system.

Administer Procurement Details

Payments to the seller

Seller compensation linked to progress

Seller performance review

Consideration for future assignments

Performing Contract Administration

Contract change control system

Buyer-conducted performance reviews and audits

Performance reporting

Payment system

Records management system

Claims Administration

Claims, disputes, or appeals

Contested changes

Disagreements

Terms of the contract

Alternative dispute resolution (ADR)

Negotiation is preferred method

CLOSE PROJECT PROCUREMENT

CLOSING PROCUREMENT IS ONE OF TWO PROJECT CLOSING PROCESSES

Contract closure is analogous to administrative closure. Its purpose is to confirm that the obligations of the contract were met as expected. The project manager, the customer, key stakeholders, and, in some instances, the seller, may finalize product verification together to confirm that the contract has been completed.

Once the vendor has completed their obligations to the contract the contract and procurement process can be closed. This lecture covers:

- Auditing the procurement process
- Closing the contract
- Updating the organizational assets

12.4 Close Procurements

Completing the procurement

Updating records to show results

Archiving contract information

Unresolved claims and litigation

Early termination
- Mutual agreement
- Default of one party
- Convenience of buyer (contractual)

ITTO: Close Procurements

Inputs	Tools & Techniques	Outputs
Project management plan	Procurement audits	Closed procurements
Procurement documents	Procurement negotiations	Organizational process assets updates
	Records management system	

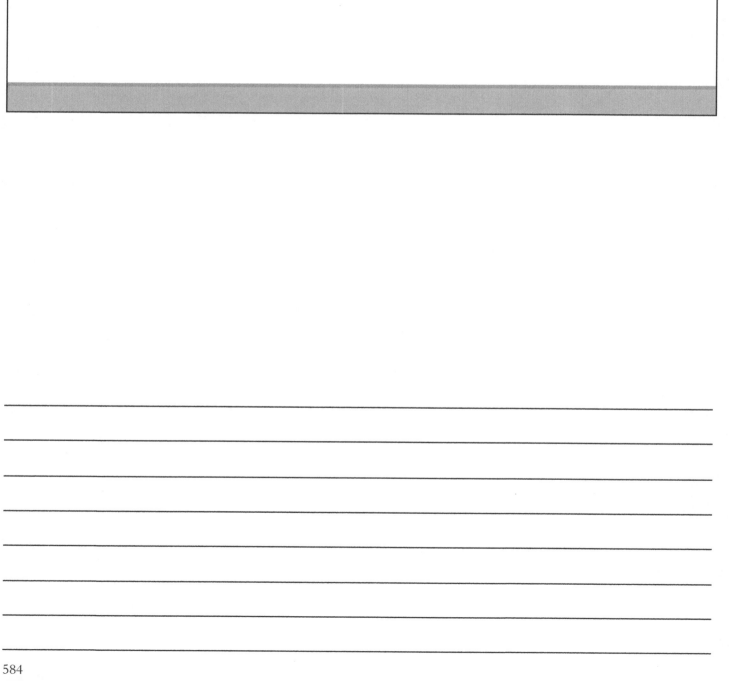

Negotiated Settlements

Equitable settlement of all outstanding

- Issues
- Disputes
- Claims
- Difference of opinion

Mediation or arbitration

Litigation in the courts

Close Procurement Outputs

Formal written notice

Procurement file

Deliverable acceptance and signoff

Lessons learned documentation

Learning Game!

http://www.instructing.com/wp-content/pub/12/story.html

Chapter exam

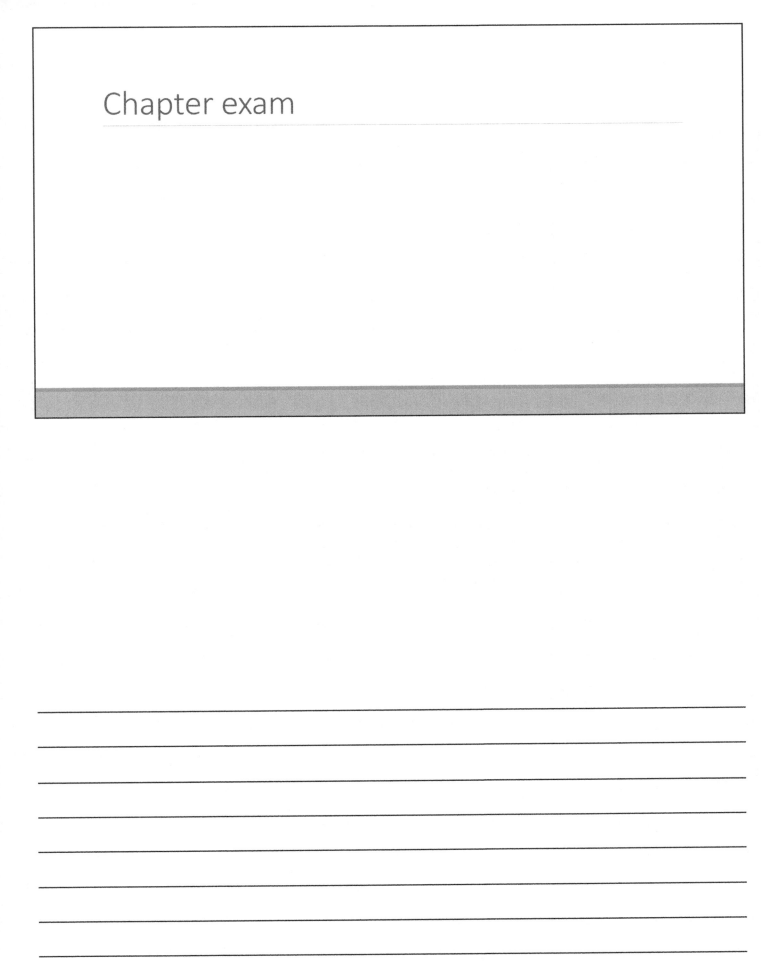

IDENTIFY PROJECT STAKEHOLDERS

IDENTIFYING, ENGAGING, AND MANAGING PROJECT STAKEHOLDERS

Stakeholder identification should happen as early as possible in the project. If you wait too long to properly identify the stakeholders, you may end up missing decisions and requirements that will only cause the project to stall, you could possibly create bad relationships with the stakeholders, and perhaps cause turmoil within the project. Stakeholder identification is a project initiating activity and requires the project manager, the project team, and other stakeholders to help identify who should be involved in the project. As you identify stakeholders, you'll classify them according to their power, influence, interests, and other characteristics so as to help you better manage the project and control stakeholder engagement. Stakeholder identification should happen as early as possible in the project. This lecture will help you determine how to best to:

- Performing stakeholder analysis
- Relying on expert judgment
- Creating the stakeholder register

13.1 Identify Stakeholders

Identifying the people, groups, organizations

Documenting stakeholder information

Defining how the stakeholders could affect the project

New knowledge area in PMBOK Guide, fifth edition

ITTO: Identify Project Stakeholders

Inputs	Tools & Techniques	Outputs
Project charter	Stakeholder analysis	Stakeholder register
Procurement documents	Expert judgment	
Enterprise environmental factors	Meetings	
Organizational process assets		

Who are stakeholders?

Persons and organizations

Involved in the project

Affected positively or negatively by project

Some can exert influence over the project

Identifying Project Stakeholders

People and groups affected by the project

Stakeholder exert influence over the project

Identify early in the project

Stakeholder management strategy

Classify stakeholders according to:
- Interest
- Influence
- Involvement

"Our greatest fear should not be of failure ... but of succeeding at things in life that don't really matter."

– Francis Chan

Stakeholder Analysis

Identify all potential stakeholders and info

Key stakeholders are

- Decision-making role
- Management role
- Primary customer

Interview stakeholders
to identify stakeholders

Stakeholder Analysis

Power/Interest Grid

Power/Influence Grid

Influence/Impact Grid

Salience model
- Power
- Urgency
- Legitimacy

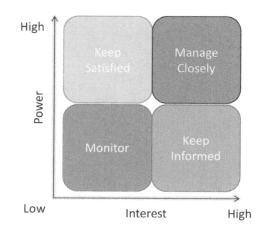

Stakeholder Register

Identification information

Assessment information

Stakeholder classification

PLAN STAKEHOLDER MANAGEMENT

CREATING A PLAN TO IDENTIFY, MANAGEMENT, AND ENGAGE STAKEHOLDERS

Stakeholder management planning helps the project manager develop a strategy to best manage the project stakeholders. This lecture defines:

- Hosting a stakeholder meeting
- Determining stakeholder influence
- Identifying stakeholder types
- Creating the Stakeholder Management Plan

13.2 Plan Stakeholder Management

Developing management strategies for stakeholder engagement

Analysis of stakeholder needs

Creates a clear plan for managing the stakeholders

13.2 Plan Stakeholder Management

Developing management strategies for stakeholder engagement

Analysis of stakeholder needs

Creates a clear plan for managing the stakeholders

ITTO: Plan Stakeholder Management

Inputs	Tools & Techniques	Outputs
Project management plan	Expert judgment	Stakeholder management plan
Stakeholder register	Meetings	Project documents updates
Enterprise environmental factors	Analytical techniques	
Organizational process assets		

_____

_____

_____

_____

_____

_____

_____

_____

Planning Stakeholder Management

Expert judgment for stakeholder management planning
- Senior management
- Project team members
- Organizational resources
- Identified key stakeholders
- Project managers
- Subject matter experts
- Regulatory bodies and nongovernmental agencies

Stakeholder Engagement Levels

Unaware

Resistant

Neutral

Supportive

Leading

Reviewing the Stakeholder Management Plan

Desired and current engagement levels

Scope and impact of change to stakeholders

Identified interrelationships and potential overlap

Stakeholder communication requirements

Information to be distributed

Reason for the distribution of that information

Time frame and frequency for the distribution of required information

MANAGE PROJECT STAKEHOLDER ENGAGEMENT

KEEPING STAKEHOLDERS ENGAGED IN THE PROJECT

As a project manager, you'll constantly work to engage the project stakeholders. You want to keep stakeholders involved and excited about the project. That's what this lecture is all about:

- Communicating with project stakeholders
- Relying on interpersonal skills
- Utilizing management skills for engagement
- Updating the project documents

13.3 Manage Stakeholder Engagement

Engaging stakeholders as needed in the project

Obtain, confirm, maintain stakeholder commitment to project

Manage stakeholder expectations

Address potential concerns

Clarifying and resolving issues

ITTO: Manage Stakeholder Engagement

Inputs	Tools & Techniques	Outputs
Stakeholder management plan	Communication methods	Issue log
Communications management plan	Interpersonal skills	Change requests
Change log	Management skills	Project management plan updates
Organizational process assets		Project documents updates
		Organizational process assets updates

Methods to Engage Stakeholders

Communication methods

Interpersonal skills
- Building trust
- Resolving conflict
- Active listening
- Overcoming resistance to change

Management skills
- Facilitate consensus
- Influence people
- Negotiate agreements
- "Modify organizational behavior to accept the project outcomes"

13.4 Control Stakeholder Engagement

Monitoring overall stakeholder relationships

Adjusting stakeholder management strategies

Updating stakeholder management plan as needed

Approach evolves as project continues

Stakeholder management is a new knowledge area in the *PMBOK Guide*, Fifth Edition. Controlling stakeholder engagement means you're controlling the stakeholder engagement throughout the project.

- Implementing a reporting system
- Maintaining stakeholder involvement
- Resolving stakeholder issues

ITTO: Control Stakeholder Engagement

Inputs	Tools & Techniques	Outputs
Project management plan	Information management systems	Work performance information
Issue log	Expert judgment	Change requests
		Project management plan updates
Work performance data	Meetings	
Project documents		Project documents updates
		Organizational process assets updates

Actively Engaging Stakeholders

Relying on information management system

Using expert judgment

Meeting with stakeholders

Being honest and direct with project news

Learning Game!

http://www.instructing.com/wp-content/pub/13/story.html

Chapter exam

ADHERE TO ETHICAL STANDARDS

PMI CODE OF ETHICS
AND PROFESSIONAL CONDUCT

The PMI Code of Ethics and Professional Responsibility is about ethics, truth, and honesty. This document is also part of your PMI Exam application process. You are required to read this document and agree to its terms as part of your testing application.

During the PMP exam, you'll be tested on these concepts:

- Complying with rules and policies
- Being an honest project manager
- Advancing the profession
- Enforcing truth and honesty
- Eliminating inappropriate actions

PMI Code of Ethics and Professional Conduct

PMI document that is part of all PMI certification applications

Must agree to its terms

Available through www.pmi.org

Responsibilities to the Profession

Organizational rules and policies
- Exam application
- Test items
- Answer sheets
- Continuing certification reporting (PDUs)

Responsibilities to the Profession

Clear and factual evidence:

- Report violations
- Cooperate with PMI on their queries
- Disclose appearance of conflict of interest

Professional Practice

Truth in advertising and sales

Comply with laws, regulations, ethical standards of country where project management is held

Advancement of Profession

Intellectual property

Disperse the code

Responsibility to Customers and to the Public

Qualifications and experience
- Truthful in experience
- Truthful in estimates (no sandbagging)

Customer is in charge

Confidentiality (privity)

Responsibility to Customers and to the Public

Avoid Conflict of Interest

Refrain from accepting inappropriate compensation
- Follow the laws and customs of the country

"We become what we think about most of the time, and that's the strangest secret."

– Earl Nightingale

Code of Conduct Extras

Sapir-Whorf Hypotheses
- ◦ understand the language

Culture shock
- ◦ Initial reaction to foreign environment

Ethnocentrism
- ◦ Measure other cultures by your own

Exam Tips

Laws of the country

Company policies

Customs

Ethics

Be an angel

What now?

Follow your study strategy

Practice your flashcards

Memorize the Memory Sheets

For additional training visit www.instructing.com

WBS Facts

The WBS is a **deliverables-based** decomposition of the project scope. Some activities are allowed in the WBS (for example, testing).

The WBS can be based on a previous project and this is a called a **WBS template**, also written as WBT.

The WBS is needed for **five project management activities**:

1. Defining project activities
2. Cost estimating
3. Cost budgeting
4. Identifying the project risks
5. Qualitative risk analysis

Scope baseline is comprised of the project scope statement, the WBS, and the WBS Dictionary.

Chart of accounts is an accounting system to track project costs by category (labor, specific materials, contractor rates). A project's chart of accounts works with the organization's chart of accounts for specific deliverables, work, and/or materials.

Code of accounts is a numbering system to identify the deliverables down to the work package within a WBS. The *PMBOK® Guide* uses a type of code of accounts: 5.3.3.2.

The **WBS dictionary** defines all of the project deliverables, resources, cost and time estimates, and associated information for each work package.

Project Selection Methods

Scoring Models

Also known as weighted scoring models, these use a common set of values to "score" each project's worthiness.

Benefit-Cost Ratios (BCRs)

This model compares benefits to costs. Consider a BCR of 4:1 versus another project of 2:5.

Future Value(FV)

How much is the Present Value (PV) worth in the future?

$$FV=PV(1+i)^n \; where:$$

FV is the value to be determined

PV is the current investment

i is the interest rate

n is the number of time periods

Present Value

How much will a future value be worth in today's dollars?

$$PV=FV/(1+i)^n \; where:$$

PV is the value to be determined

FV is the promised return on investment

i is the interest rate

n is the number of time periods

Net Present Value

This formula finds the present value on the project for each year the project promises a return:

1. Each time period's promised return is calculated into present value.
2. Sum all of the time periods' present value.
3. Subtract the project's original investment from the sum.
4. An NPV greater than one is good, less than one is bad.

Constrained Optimization Methods

Complex formulas to determine a project's worthiness to be selected. Examples include:

- Linear programming
- Nonlinear programming
- Integer algorithms
- Dynamic programming
- Multiobjective programming

Project Purpose

Projects are chartered to give the project manager the authority to act on behalf of the project sponsor or customer.

Projects are chartered to solve a problem or seize an opportunity.

Project selection is part of an organization's portfolio management process.

Managing the Project Change Control Components

Project Management Information System

All changes must be documented and entered into the **PMIS**. There are four change control systems (CCS). Scope changes go on to the **configuration management system** for features and functions documentation. All changes pass through **integrated change control**. The relevant project components are updated based on the change that has occurred.

- Scope CCS
- Schedule CCS
- Cost CCS
- Contract CCS

Configuration Management System *(Only scope changes)*

Integrated Change Control

- Product Scope
- Project Scope
- WBS
- WBS Dictionary
- Project Plan

How to Calculate Float

Complete the Forward Pass

1. The Early Start (ES) of the first task is one. The Early Finish (EF) is a task's ES, plus the duration, minus one.
2. The ES of the next task(s) will be the EF for the previous activity, plus one.
3. The EF for the next task(s) equals its ES, plus the task duration, minus one.
4. Use caution with predecessor activities; the EF with the largest value is carried forward.

Complete the Backward Pass

1. Backward pass starts at the end of the PND. The Late Finish (LF) for the last activity in the PND equals its EF value. The Late Start (LS) is calculated by subtracting the duration of the activity from its LF, plus one.
2. The next predecessor activity's LF equals the LS of the successor activity minus one.
3. The LS is again calculated by subtracting the task's duration from the task's LF, plus one.

Calculate Float

1. To calculate float, the ES is subtracted from the LS and the EF is subtracted from the LF. The following illustration shows a completed PND with the float exposed.

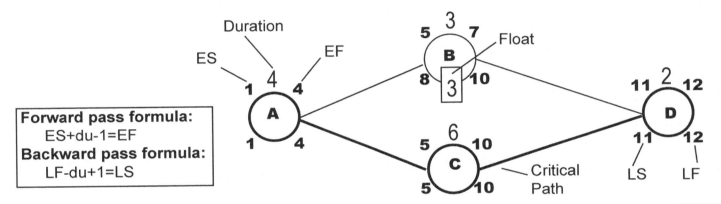

Time Facts

Lag: Waiting time between activities (positive time).

Lead: Activities are moved closer together or even overlap (negative time).

Crashing: Adding resources to reduce the project duration. This adds costs to the project.

Fast tracking: Allows project phases to overlap to reduce the project duration. This adds risk to the project.

Free float: The amount of time an activity can be delayed without delaying the next activity's start date.

Total float: The amount of time an activity can be delayed without delaying the project's end date.

Float: An opportunity to delay an activity. Also called slack.

Task Relationships

Finish-to-start (FS): This relationship means Task A must complete before Task B can begin. This is the most common relationship.

Start-to-start (SS): This relationship means Task A must start before Task B can start. This relationship allows both activities to happen in tandem.

Finish-to-finish (FF): This relationship means Task A must complete before Task B does. Ideally, two tasks must finish at exactly the same time, but this is not always the case.

Start-to-finish (SF): This relationship is unusual and is rarely used. It requires Task A to start so that Task B may finish. It is also known as just-in-time (JIT) scheduling.

Miscellaneous Time Facts

Three-point estimate: This time estimate approach uses three factors to predict the duration of each task. The formula is (optimistic + most likely + pessimistic) divided by three. It is an average of the three time factors for each activity.

PERT (Program Evaluation and Review Technique): This approach is weighted on the most likely estimate. The formula is the optimistic, plus four times the most likely, plus the pessimistic; this sum is then divided by six. I like to write this as (O + (4ML) + P)/6.

Critical chain: Network diagramming approach based on the availability of project resources to determine project completion. Uses buffers (feeding buffers) of time instead of project float.

Earned Value Management

Name	Formula	Mnemonic Device
Planned Value	% planned completion	Please
Earned Value	% complete x BAC	Eat
Cost Variance	CV=EV-AC	Carl's
Schedule Variance	SV=EV-PV	Sugar
Cost Performance Index	CPI=EV/AC	Candy
Schedule Performance Index	SPI=EV/PV	S (*this and the next two spell SEE*)
Estimate at Completion	EAC=BAC/CPI	E
Estimate to Complete	ETC=EAC-AC	E
To-Complete Performance Index (Using BAC)	(BAC-EV)/(BAC-AC)	The
To-Complete Performance Index (Using EAC)	(BAC-EV)/(EAC-AC)	Taffy
Variance at Completion	VAC=BAC-EAC	Violin

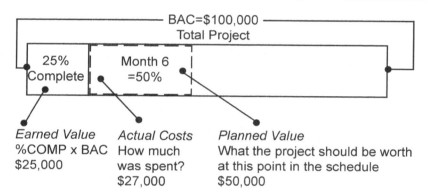

Earned Value
%COMP x BAC
$25,000

Actual Costs
How much
was spent?
$27,000

Planned Value
What the project should be worth
at this point in the schedule
$50,000

Five EVM Rules to Memorize

. Always start with earned value.

. Variance means subtraction.

. Indexes are "something" divided by "something" and they show performance for the project objectives.

. When it comes to any index, the closer to 1 the better.

. Variances can be positive or negative.

Project Cost Types

Variable costs: The cost of the deliverable, service, or materials can fluctuate based on varying factors.

Fixed costs: A constant "fixed" cost throughout the project.

Indirect costs: An expense that can be shared with other projects or the organization, such as rent, phone, or equipment.

Direct costs: Costs that are directly tied to the project.

Sunk costs are monies that have been invested into a project. Sunk costs are gone, they are "sunk" into a project.

An **opportunity cost** is the amount of an opportunity that is given up. Consider: Project A is worth $55,000 and Project B is worth $89,000, you'd choose Project B to do. The opportunity is $55,000—the amount of Project A that you can't do because of the opportunity of Project B.

Estimate Types

Rough order of magnitude: Simple, early estimate. Range of variance is -25% to +75% for the project completion.

Budget estimate: Early planning estimate and/or top-down approach. Range of variance is -10% to +25% for the project completion.

Definitive estimate: Most accurate estimate, but takes longest to complete; uses the bottom-up approach. Range of variance is -5% to +10% for the project completion.

Bottom-up: Requires a WBS and accounts for each work package.

Analogous: Creates an analogy between projects; also known as a top-down estimate.

Parametric: Uses a parameter (cost per ton, cost per unit) for the estimate.

Quality Costs

Cost of quality is the cost to achieve the expected quality on a project. Consider training, safety, and materials.

Cost of poor quality, also known as the cost of nonconformance to quality, is the cost of not achieving quality: rework, loss of life or limb, loss of sales.

Don't change your answers. Most people change correct answers to wrong answers.

Project Management Charts and Values

Run Chart

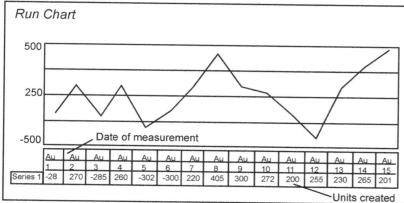

	Au 1	Au 2	Au 3	Au 4	Au 5	Au 6	Au 7	Au 8	Au 9	Au 10	Au 11	Au 12	Au 13	Au 14	Au 15
Series 1	-28	270	-285	260	-302	-300	220	405	300	272	200	255	230	265	201

Units created

Control Chart

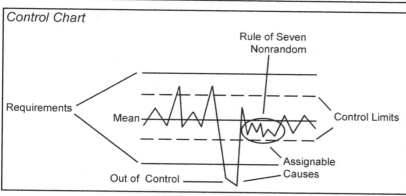

Cause-and-Effect Chart
Also Called Fishbone and Ishikawa Chart

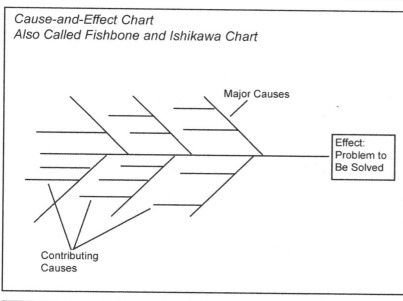

Pareto Chart

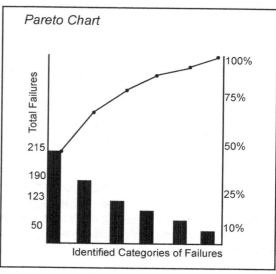

Normal Distribution

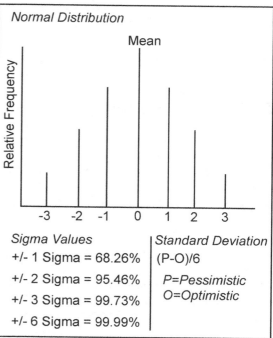

Sigma Values
+/- 1 Sigma = 68.26%
+/- 2 Sigma = 95.46%
+/- 3 Sigma = 99.73%
+/- 6 Sigma = 99.99%

Standard Deviation
(P-O)/6

P=Pessimistic
O=Optimistic

Hard questions and easy questions are worth the same: one point. Don't spend too much time laboring over a question. Choose an answer, mark it for review, and then move on.

Quality Facts

Quality is a conformance to requirements and a fitness for use. It is fulfilling the project scope.

Grade is a category or rank given to entities having the same functional use but different technical characteristics.

Gold plating is the process of adding extra features to drive up costs and consume the budget.

Quality assurance is a *prevention-driven* process to do the project work right the first time.

Quality control is an *inspection-driven* process to keep mistakes from entering the customers' hands.

Scope creep is the addition of small, undocumented changes that bypass the scope change control system. Scope creep is sometimes called **project poison**.

A **scatter diagram** is like a run chart, but it instead tracks the relationship between two variables. The two variables are considered related the closer they track against a diagonal line. Consider the relationship of costs and schedule.

Project Management Professional Theories

Maslow's Hierarchy of Needs
Maslow believed that we have five needs; we're on a quest to satisfy these needs. The needs are, from the bottom up:

Physiological. We need air, food, clothing, and shelter.
Safety. We need safety and security.
Social. We need friends, approval, and love.
Esteem. We need respect, appreciation, and approval.
Self-actualization. We need personal growth, knowledge, and fulfillment.

Herzberg's Theory of Motivation
There are hygiene agents and motivating agents.
Hygiene agents are expectations for employment: paycheck, insurance, safe working environment.
Motivating agents are motivators for employees such as bonuses, career advancement, opportunity to grow. Hygiene agents will not motivate, but their absence will demotivate.

Halo Effect
All opinions are formed by one component. A great engineer doesn't always make a great project manager.

Parkinson's Law
Individuals allow their work to consume all of their time. Work will expand to fill the amount of time allotted to it.

McGregor's X and Y
Management's perspective of employees. X people are bad, lazy, and need to be micromanaged. Y people are self-directed. Most managers have X and Y attributes.

Ouchi's Theory Z
Workers do well if motivated. This provides participative management, familial work environment, and lifelong employment. Known as Japanese Management Style.

McClelland's Theory of Needs
Needs are acquired over time and are shaped by life experiences. Our needs are categorized as achievement, affiliation, and power. McClelland used a Thematic Apperception Test (TAT) to determine an individual's needs.

Vroom's Expectancy Theory
People behave based on what they believe (expect) their behavior to bring them.

PMI HR Terms

Role: This person is accountable by the title they possess (network engineer, business analyst).
Responsibility: The owner of the assigned work is accountable for the work.
Authority: Based on organizational structure; autonomy to make decisions, approvals, and manage resources.

Stakeholder Identification

Stakeholder analysis: This is a three-step process of identifying the project stakeholders early in the project, identify the impact/support of each stakeholder, and then plan how to influence stakeholders to act in given situations.

Stakeholder register: Documents stakeholder identification, assessment of influence, and stakeholder type.

Stakeholder classification models: These are grids to plot out stakeholder power, influence, and interest in the project. Here are four common models:

Power/interest grid - how much power/interest do the stakeholders have?

Power/influence grid - how much power/influence do the stakeholders have?

Influence/impact grid - how much influence (involvement of decisions) and impact on project change do the stakeholders have?

Salience model - classifies stakeholders based on power, urgency, and legitimacy for the project.

Project Manager Powers

Expert: The authority of the project manager comes from experience with the technology the project focuses on.

Reward: The project manager has the authority to reward the project team.

Formal: The project manager has been assigned by senior management and is in charge of the project. Also known as **positional power**.

Coercive: The project manager has the authority to discipline the project team members. This is also known as "**penalty power**."

Referent: The project team personally knows the project manager. Referent can also mean the project manager refers to the person who assigned him the position.

Conflict Management

Problem solving: Both parties work together for the good of the project in a spirit of problem solving. Also known as confronting. This is a **win-win** solution.

Compromising: Both parties give up something, often in a heated scenario. This is a **lose-lose** solution.

Forcing: One party quickly forces their solution over another. Often done by seniority. This is a **win-lose** solution.

Withdrawal (also known as avoidance): One party leaves the discussion. This is a **yield-lose** solution.

Smoothing: The differences of the problem are downplayed. This is a delay and is a **lose-lose** solution.

Be careful who sees the stakeholder management strategy because it may contain sensitive information.

Project Communications Management Facts

Communication channels formula: $N(N-1)/2$, where N represents the number of stakeholders.

55% of communication is nonverbal.

Paralingual: the pitch, tone, inflection of the speaker that affects the content of the message.

Effective listening: watching the speaker's body language, interpreting paralingual clues, asking questions for clarity, and offering feedback.

Active listening: participating in the conversation through verbal and nonverbal signs of message receipt.

Messages are **transmitted**; knowledge is **transferred**.

Acknowledgment of a message doesn't mean acceptance of the message.

Communications Model

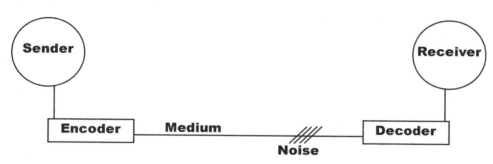

The **sender** sends the message and it is **encoded**. The **medium** transfers the message. The **decoder** decodes the message for the **receiver**. **Noise** on the medium could interfere with the message. **Barriers** prevent communication from happening. An **acknowledgment** of the message doesn't mean agreement with the message. Communication happens when information is **transferred**.

Risk Responses

Avoidance: Avoid the risk.

Mitigation: Reduce the probability or impact of the risk event.

Acceptance: The risk may be small so the risk may be accepted.

Transference: The ownership of the risk is transferred to some other party, usually for a fee.

Exploit: A positive risk that a project wants to take advantage of.

Share: A positive risk that can be shared with the organization or other projects.

Enhance: A response that ensures that a positive risk will likely happen.

Risk Terms

Contingency fund: An amount of funds used to offset a project's risks.

Secondary risks: A risk response creates another risk.

Residual risks: A risk response may create small generally accepted risks.

Triggers: Condition, event, or warning sign that a risk is about to happen. Usually "triggers" a risk response.

Positive risk: Risks with a positive impact.

Negative risks: Risks with a negative impact.

Pure risk: Only offers a negative impact (injury, fire, theft, destruction).

Business risk: Risks that can offer an upside or a downside (both positive and/or negative impacts). .

Qualitative analysis: Qualifying the risks for their legitimacy. This is a very quick, subjective approach.

Quantitative analysis: Quantifies the risk exposure based on evidence, research, and in-depth analysis of the risk events.

Utility function: A person's or organization's willingness to accept risk.
Relative to the project priority as high-priority projects are typically risk adverse. Also known as risk tolerance.

Quantitative Risk Matrix

Risk	Probability	Impact	Ex$V
A	.60	-$10,000	-$6,000
B	.20	-25,000	-5,000
C	.40	-40,000	-16,000
D	.10	35,000	3,500
Risk exposure			**-$23,500**
Contingency reserve			**$23,500**

The **risks** are identified and recorded in the **risk register**. The **probability** of each risk is found as is the risk **impact**. The probability times the impact equates to the **Expected Monetary Value (Ex$V)**. Some risks can have a positive impact. The sum of the Ex$V is the **risk exposure**. The positive opposite of the risk exposure is the amount needed for the **contingency reserve**.

Procurement Terms

Contracts: An offer and consideration. Contracts are backed by the court system.

Cost reimbursable contracts: Risk is with the buyer as the buyer pays for cost overruns.

Fixed-price (lump-sum contracts): Risk is with the seller as seller pays for cost overruns.

Time and materials contract: Buyer pays for the time and materials of the vendor. Must have a **not-to-exceed** (NTE) clause.

Purchase order: A unilateral form of a contract.

Letter of intent: The buyer tells the vendor they intend to do business with them; not a binding agreement.

Letter contract: Generally short-term purchase used as a stopgap or emergency response.

Bidder conference: Vendors all meet with the buyer to discuss the details of the statement of work so they may prepare a bid, quote, or proposal.

Procurement Process

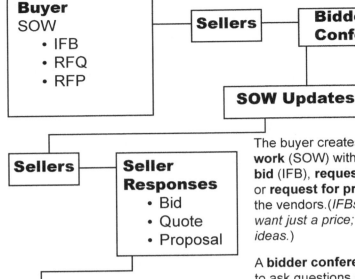

The buyer creates a **statement of work** (SOW) with an **invitation for bid** (IFB), **request for quote** (RFQ), or **request for proposal** (RFP) for the vendors.(*IFBs and RFQs both want just a price; a proposal wants ideas.*)

A **bidder conference** allows sellers to ask questions about the SOW. The buyer may create an updated SOW to give back to the sellers that attended the bidder conference.

Sellers respond with a **bid**, **quote**, or **proposal**. The buyer completes seller selection and creates a **contract**.

Decentralized contracting is done by the PM; centralized contracting is done with a purchasing agent or through a central procurement office.

Organizational Structures

Projectized

- PM has the most authority.
- Team is typically assigned to the project full-time.
- Competition between teams may hurt the organization.
- Team is uncertain of future work after the project is completed.
- PM is full-time and has full-time administrative staffing.

Strong Matrix

- PM has strong authority.
- Typical full-time resources from functional departments.
- Internal competition may increase for resources.
- Project team members are on multiple projects.
- PM is full-time and has full-time administrative staffing.

Balanced Matrix

- PM and functional managers balance power.
- Power struggles are common. Internal competition may increase for resources.
- Project team members are on multiple projects.
- PM is full-time and has part-time administrative staffing.

Weak Matrix

- PM has less power than functional managers.
- Internal competition may increase for resources.
- Project team members are on multiple projects.
- PM is part-time and has part-time administrative staffing.

Functional

- PM has little authority.
- Organization is structured by departments or functions (sales, manufacturing, IT, etc.).
- PM may be called a project coordinator or expeditor.
- The functional manager has all of the authority.
- Focus is on completing the project work along with day-to-day work.
- PM is part-time and has part-time administrative staffing.

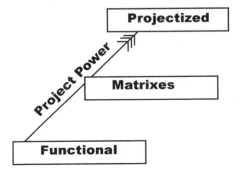

Organizational structure affects questions; pay attention to who has the power.

47 Processes and 10 Knowledge Areas

Knowledge Areas	Process Groups				
	Initiating - 2	Planning - 24	Executing - 8	M&C - 11	Closing - 2
Project Integration Management	Develop project charter	Develop project management plan	Direct and manage project work	Monitor and control project work Integrated change control	Close project or phase
Project Scope Management		Plan scope management Collect requirements Define scope Create WBS		Validate scope Control scope	
Project Time Management		Plan schedule management Define activities Sequence activities Estimate activity resources Estimate activity durations Develop schedule		Control schedule	
Project Cost Management		Plan cost management Estimate costs Determine budget		Control costs	
Project Quality Management		Plan quality management	Quality assurance	Control quality	
Project HR Management		Plan HR management	Acquire team Develop team Manage team		
Project Communication Management		Communications planning	Manage communications	Control communications	
Project Risk Management		Plan risk management Identify risk Perform qualitative risk analysis Perform quantitative risk analysis Plan risk responses		Control risks	
Project Procurement Management		Plan procurement management	Conduct procurements	Control procurements	Close procurements
Project Stakeholder Management	Identify stakeholders	Plan stakeholder management	Manage stakeholder engagement	Control stakeholder engagement	

Spend time on Initiating, Executing, and Closing. There are few processes, but many questions. Work smart, not hard.

629

Instructing.com, LLC

PMI Registered Education Provider #4082

44227307R00349

Made in the USA
Middletown, DE
04 May 2019